The Golden Rule
Of Epistemology
And Other Essays

by Anthony Horvath

I0143084

Published by

ATHANATOS
PUBLISHING GROUP

The Golden Rule Of Epistemology And Other Essays
by Anthony Horvath

Published by Athanatos Publishing Group

www.athanatosministries.org

Cover Design by Julius Broqueza.

ISBN: 978-1-936830-84-8

Table of Contents

Foreword

Most of what follows has never been published before, either online or in print. The two exceptions are the brief piece on what to do when churches are not sympathetic to apologetics, which was first made available to Brian Auten at the Apologia315 blog, and the piece on homosexuality, which was published on my own blog, at sntjohnny.com. This particular piece was originally written in response to some inquiries by some atheist friends but also some Christians. I have edited it with a more general audience in mind.

I have made reference to my 'golden rule of epistemology' for nearly twenty years. It would not be too far at all to say that it is this line of thinking that brought me from a state of unbelief to the conviction that there is a God, and that Christianity is the most accurate and likely account for who he is. Of course, the actual progression in my own life was not nearly as orderly as presented here.

A brief word on 'epistemology' may be in order.

Epistemology is essentially the study of how we know that what we know is really true. It may surprise some people to learn that the core of that word, is the Greek word *pistos,* which is interpreted variously as 'faith' or 'believing.' Many people do not see faith as having any connection to actual knowledge!

Pistos, in turn, comes from the word *peitho*, which means 'to persuade' or 'to prevail upon.' For those accustomed to seeing 'faith' in entirely pejorative terms, it may be disconcerting to learn that biblical 'faith' is a much more robust term than 'free-thinkers' ever imagined.

The truth is that in the classical sense of the original Greek word, there is no hint of 'blind faith.' The authors of the Gospels had no intention of invoking *that* idea when they used the word,[1] nor did any of the other New Testament writers. They use the word deliberately, to call upon the

---

[1] See John 20:27, as an example.

reader to make *a considered investigation* into their claims. This is a far cry from what atheists perceive is being done when Jesus calls upon them to 'believe.'[2]

But probably, the word 'faith' is as badly understood by Christians as it is, non-Christians. In my piece on Lutheran baptism, this is alluded to, but not dwelt on. There is a very real sense in which faith in Christ is understood to be something propositional, when in fact, it is *positional*. It is about *where you are* more than it is the things you believe.

My sense is that people put things into separate boxes when in fact it is often the case that the things are inseparable. Reading this collection from beginning to end, I believe the reader will notice how similar ideas surface throughout. Despite the fact that these essays were written over a period of ten years, none of them with an eye towards any of the others, it will become evident that I firmly believe that there are more things inseparable than there are things that can be taken in isolation.

It is my hope that this collection of essays serve as the starting point for people across the spectrum to take a fresh look at ideas and concepts that they thought they fully understood. Once seen under different light, it is my further hope that they will shed new light in other areas—perhaps areas the reader has struggled to make sense of, whether that reader be Christian, or non-Christian.

    − Anthony Horvath, PhD−

---

[2] The Greek word translated as 'believe' is the same as the one for 'faith' which is the same as the one for 'to persuade.' *Pistos.*

By GUM, there is a God, and we are not Him!
Anthony Horvath's "Golden Rule of Epistemology" And Implications Thereof
PART ONE:
THE RULE
A Brief Overview of the Golden Rule

Rule #1 of Epistemology: Any argument utilizing reason that concludes that reason is illusory, false, inherently unreliable, etc., must be rejected out-of-hand. Corollary: only arguments that uphold the general integrity of reason can be considered.

Here is a statement that should be self-evident and obvious to anyone and everyone but seems to escape the notice of the geniuses among us, even though the general idea is part of our cultural currency, reflected in such phrases as "do not saw off the limb you are standing on." Epistemology is, roughly speaking, the study of how we know what we know and why we think what we know is really true. If through this study you conclude that we cannot know things or what we think we know can't be deemed trustworthy, obviously—or, one would think it would be obvious—this conclusion itself should fall under the knife. The 'golden rule of epistemology' clearly follows: any conclusion we make that calls into question the validity of our ability to draw reasonable conclusions must be categorically rejected.

Epistemology covers a wide range of human experience: the brain, the mind, the body, the senses, and so on. At the core of our epistemology, however, is what mediates it all: *our reason.* It is meaningless and incoherent to speak of 'knowing' anything without using our reason, so the 'golden rule' applies to our 'reasoning' in particular, even as it relates to the whole human experience in general.

Thus, the 'golden rule' *necessarily* implies that if, *by your use of reason*, you throw into doubt reason itself, *it must be the case* that something has gone horribly awry in your reasoning. Logically, if you accept the validity of the Golden Rule, you are left with two basic choices: 1. toss out the offending argument altogether or, 2. content yourself with a life of *a*-rationality.

We cannot even say *irrationality*, because 'irrationality' at least presumes that there is such a thing as 'rationality' which can be violated, but those who subvert reason *itself* are no longer in the domain of rationality at all. Yet I said that you are *logically* left with two basic choices. The people we tend to find who violate the Golden Rule are, by definition, not bound by logic at all, which leaves them free to select choice number 3: "Ignore the fact that your argument undermined reason itself and proceed unbothered." They understand the implications of their argument, but just don't care.

There is yet another path open to the one who violates the Golden Rule, but it is not a choice, *per se*. In this scenario, the person has arrived at a position by the use of reason that guts the integrity of reason itself but is wholly unaware of this fact. It is a sorry state of affairs, but true nonetheless, that we find this path taken most often by people who insist they are the most reasonable people among us and the true guardians of logical thought.

The Golden Rule thus serves as a cautionary tale for all of us as we attempt to map out our surroundings and understand them. There are many ways of violating the Golden Rule. For example, for the theist, some versions of the doctrine of Total Depravity commit it, for if our reason was entirely compromised we could not reasonably conclude that it was entirely compromised. There are also instances where it seems that the Golden Rule is far from sight when in fact it is near at hand. Even for the one sensitive to upholding the Golden Rule, it is possible to encounter its applicability unexpectedly.

That said, the most common violator of this principle is the atheist, and he is usually to be counted among those who don't even know what they've done, rather than one who knows but just doesn't care.

PART TWO:
THE RULE'S APPLICATION TO ATHEISM
How the Atheist Remains Oblivious

There are, of course, atheists that have wrestled with the mysterious fact that reason is reasonable, but in the main, materialists aren't even aware of the mystery at all. If presented with the issue, they are quick to point out that they, and we, have no choice but to accept that reason is reasonable. But surely *this fact* requires some explanation, some accounting for in our worldview?

Moreover, just because it is true that we must proceed as though reason is efficacious, shouldn't it be obvious that we shouldn't *by* our reasoning conclude that reason is not reliable? If 'epistemology' is the 'science' of studying how we know that what we know is true and accurate, surely we must acknowledge that the whole process hinges on the legitimacy of reason itself, by which we carry out our study? If the roots of reason are pulled out, knowledge itself withers on the vine. It would behoove us, then, to be careful not to disturb reason from its foundations, and moreover include in our perspective an explanation for *why* reason 'works' and *why* we shouldn't disturb it from its foundations!

We must take it as axiomatic that the very best worldview will be the one that maximally incorporates the aspects of reality and ties them together coherently. Given a choice between a worldview that accounts for *why* "reason is reasonable" and one that merely takes it for granted, the former should be preferred. The latter may conceivably be coherent, but if it refuses to explain why "reason is reasonable" we have good cause to be unimpressed; tidy systems are easy to create when you exclude from

3

consideration the really mysterious and difficult to understand aspects of human experience.

The atheist builds his worldview on the assumption that reason is reasonable but declines to offer an explanation for this fact, and substitutes in its place the justification that we have no choice. It is true, we have no choice, but that only highlights the need to make sure that our reason does not undermine reason. However, what tends to happen is that the refusal to pay attention to this question results in conclusions that do undermine the integrity of reason, but with the person totally unaware of what he has done.

He is oblivious because in his mind, the two things are kept in two separate boxes. In one box, which he never opens, looks at, thinks about, or even sparks his curiosity, is the necessary fact that *reason is reasonable*. In the other box are presuppositions, empirical discoveries, musings, and so forth, which he feels free to move around indiscriminately as though they were toys. These playthings are considered as part of an entirely different system which is to be interpreted only in reference to itself.

Through this mental maneuver, the atheist tends not to realize that the conclusions he builds from the materials in the latter box would contradict the realities in the former box. But in reality, there is only one 'box' and there *can* only be one 'box.' Only in pretend-world are there two.

What the Atheist is Afraid Of: the Singularity of Reason

Now, materialistic outlooks have tended to simply take "reason is reasonable" for granted, but there have been exceptions. Atheistic philosophers such as Bertrand Russell, Ayers, and Hume, are examples of materialists who know that Reason is itself a phenomenon that requires some explanation and account.

The problem is that the thing to be explained needs to be accounted for from a 'third person' perspective—from the 'outside looking in,' as it were—but we are thoroughly intertwined and enmeshed with the thing to be explained. We *cannot* assess reason without *using* reason. It would be as if we were a water molecule wishing to gauge the speed and direction of the current of the river we were flowing within; without a frame of reference, we cannot establish anything absolute. The thing to be done requires standing on the shore, which we cannot do, by virtue of the fact that we are a water molecule; that is, we cannot do the thing required, *by definition*.

To put it another way, the thing to be done can only be done from a frame of reference that *transcends* our own.

And if there is anything a materialist cannot abide, it is *anything* that is transcendental! If even one thing is determined to be real, but transcends matter, *that is immaterial*, this disproves materialism. For this reason, then, naturally, the materialist steadfastly refuses to consider options that would account for the reasonableness of reason that transcend matter itself.

This poses a significant problem since one of the few facts that humanity shares as most basic, and knows most intimately, is the *prima facie* transcendental nature of logic. The law of non-contradiction cannot be discovered in rocks or by careful mixing of chemicals. That a square cannot *by definition* be a circle is an immaterial fact that would be the case in any possible universe. Despite the self-evident understanding that logic and reasoning is immaterial if it is anything, many people are hell-bent on denying their plain experience of reality, and seek for ways of reducing reason to rock, dirt, and flame.

The fruits of this approach are all variations on a theme that have all been exposed as failures, usually because they either refute themselves or stand as axiomatic as the axioms they mean 'explain.'

For example, Hume's empiricism cannot be empirically proven. Similarly, the verification principle cannot itself be verified. The assertion one sometimes hears that 'free will' is an illusion and that everything is wholly determined must, on that same view, be wholly determined, since one could not have said otherwise. These materialistic efforts flatly contradicted themselves and only yield 'results' by swapping out one axiom for another. When the principles were turned onto themselves, the result was absurdity at worst, and tautology at best.

All attempts to 'get behind' reason devolve into a singularity, of sorts. Just as the scientists relying solely on the laws of nature finally arrived at a point, less than a second after the 'Big Bang,' when the laws of nature themselves no longer hold and it is impossible—*by definition*—to peer further back than the singularity that is the beginning of the universe itself, so too the materialist philosophers cannot get beyond the laws of thought to the external origin and basis for those laws of thought: a Singularity of Reason.

What the Atheist Cannot Tolerate: GUM

Indeed, the best course of action for such philosophers would be to posit the reasonableness of reason as The Great Unanswerable Mystery (GUM), conceding to the world that here, at least, is something that they will never *in principle* be able to explain. However, a GUM such as this would leave the great mass of humanity ample justification to look beyond materialism to *non-materialistic* accounts for our existence and reality itself—and there is nothing an atheist hates more than *even the notion* that anyone could reasonably be anything other than an atheist. See Dawkins, Dennett, and the 'new' atheists for evidence of this assertion.

Because of this inability to account for the reasonableness of reason and the extremely dim prospects of ever being able to see beyond the Singularity of Reason, atheists have turned to the weapons that have historically given them the best results: ridicule, insult, slander. In other words, to even suggest that one should be curious about the 'reasonableness of reason' or insist that the superior worldview would be the one that accounts for it is met with angry denouncements, as if the validity of their position is self-evident to any reasonable person. If the reader doubts this, they may raise the question in the atheistic forum of their choice, and see how it goes.

To be fair, though, atheistic philosophers will tend to be more sympathetic to critics. However, since most atheists claim the mantle of 'science' and empiricism, most will be content to point out that reason is vindicated enough by the fact that we put a man on the moon—and you are an idiot for thinking that this is insufficient evidence of the reasonableness of reason—never mind the fact that it was not *the fact* that reason is reasonable that was being questioned in the first place. Reason *is* reasonable... but *why* and *how*?

Theoretically, if materialists would be willing to openly acknowledge that a GUM serves as the foundation of their worldview, they could proceed to build the rest of their worldview in a manner that did not gut their GUM, and hence bring their worldview toppling down around them once the issue of the reasonableness of reason was raised. I'm not sure what kind of atheistic worldview would result from such an open acknowledgement, but as I have submitted, we are not likely to see anything of the sort anytime soon. This is unfortunate, because their refusal to deal honestly with this GUM leads them to take positions that implicitly and explicitly undermine reason itself.

I am willing to leave it open as conceivable that some materialist may someday openly admit to Singularity of Reason and create a system that does not simultaneously war against that Singularity. On this view, it would take the Singularity for granted without attempting to explain or account for it, but it would be cognizant of that fact and work hard to make sure that whatever came later wouldn't undermine it. In my opinion, such a worldview would be inferior to the one that *could* explain and account for the reasonableness of reason, but at least the materialists would have something that is internally consistent and coherent. As it stands, however, contemporary materialism tends to take reason for granted without admitting that it is doing so, and then proceeds to entertain a number of propositions that render the worldview incoherent and inconsistent.

That is to say, if materialism is true—on present materialistic grounds—*we could not know it is true*. Or anything, for that matter. Wherever one turns, modern materialism violates what I call the Golden Rule of Epistemology.

How Materialism Fundamentally Violates the Golden Rule

We may touch on one of the most basic examples, as concerns the nature of the universe. C.S. Lewis puts the problem this way:

> Supposing there was no intelligence behind the universe, no creative mind. In that case, nobody designed my brain for the purpose of thinking. It is merely that when the atoms inside my skull happen, for physical or chemical reasons, to arrange themselves in a certain way, this gives me, as a by-product, the sensation I call thought. But, if so, how can I trust my own thinking to be true? It's like upsetting a milk jug and hoping the way it splashes itself will give you a map of London. But if I can't trust my own thinking, of course I can't trust the arguments leading to Atheism, and therefore have no reason to be an Atheist, or anything else. Unless I believe in God, I cannot believe in thought; so I can never use thought to disbelieve in God. [The Case for Christianity, p. 32]

Set aside, for now, Lewis's progression to the necessity of believing in God as the escape for the materialist's conundrum. Focus, instead, just on that conundrum. On the materialist's view, mind = brain, and brain = matter, and matter = atoms, all the way down to whatever one wishes to suppose is the rock bottom particulate, whatever one wishes

8

to call it. The materialist believes that once one has reached this point, they've exhausted all of what is real, and *everything* is composed somehow of *this.*

Now, *this*, whatever it is, has somehow arranged itself so that we experience (or so we think) self-awareness and what we call 'mind.' But of course it hasn't 'arranged itself' because that phrase presupposes an 'arranger,' some kind of intelligent purposing. On this view, there isn't intelligence, there is just *stuff.* On what grounds can we suppose that the particular arrangement of atoms that give us the appearance of 'thought' *actually* corresponds and correlates to reality as it really is? We may just as easily suppose that reality actually is some other way than we perceive it. Our perceptions are nothing more than a 'brain state,' which is to say, some arrangement of the underlying stuff of the universe. For all we know, the pencil on our desk is having the exact same thoughts. Maybe the pencil regards *us* as the writing instrument! Maybe pencils and writing instruments and desks and 'us' are all just 'brain states,' where a 'brain state' is just a particular configuration of that rock bottom 'stuff' that the universe consists of. Wait a minute; according to materialism that is precisely what they, and 'we,' are!

The fact that we have no choice but to rely on our sense that we experience these 'brain states' as acts of reasoning doesn't obviate the fact that on this view, there is no fundamental distinction between this or that atomic state, anywhere else in the universe. In short, you cannot get *mind* from *mindless matter*, and materialism leaves no quarter for any other mind that is not made from similar *stuff.*

Some analogies can help us understand just what kind of predicament materialism puts us in.

Imagine, if you will, that you are playing a dice game, such as Yahtzee®. As the reader likely knows, this game requires five six-sided dice, and the goal is to get as many rolls with matching results as possible. One gets three rolls to get a five-of-a-kind (and if you get it, you are supposed to yell, "Yahtzee®!") but it is so improbable that one tends to go for more likely arrangements, such as three fours, or a 'full house' and what not. Yet, it is not so improbable as to be impossible. It is actually possible to get a Yahtzee® on a single roll.

Moreover, the odds are such that if you had an infinite number of rolls, it is *practically* impossible to *never* get a Yahtzee®. While the odds of getting one in a single roll is 1 in 7,776, as one proceeds, keeping the dice that match (say, keeping all of the 'threes'), eventually one will get down to having 4 'threes,' and then with just one die left, your odds are 1 in 6. While it is conceivably possible that one can roll that die forever without getting your last 'three,' in reality you will have your Yahtzee® within a few minutes.

Now, if you were the one doing the rolling of the dice, you would know precisely how many rolls it actually took to get your Yahtzee®. For illustration's sake, let us suppose it took 100 tries. Now suppose that you became bored with rolling dice, so you leave the room. A few minutes later, a friend enters the room and sees the dice on the table with all five still showing their 'threes.' Does your friend have any way to determine, whatsoever, whether you obtained your Yahtzee® in 1 try versus 3 tries, versus 100 tries?

He does not—unless you reveal it to him. Then, of course, since your friend wasn't a direct witness, whether or not he 'knows' how many rolls it took depends in large part on your credibility with him.

At any rate, here we have a 'particulate' with 6 possible eventualities, but as you can see from this illustration, it is impossible, judging from the state of the particulates *themselves*, to distinguish between an arrangement arrived at after 100 successive tries and one arrived at after just 1 try.

But now imagine that you are not the friend, but rather *the dice*. Since your brain, nay, your entire being, consists solely of mindless 'particulates,' you also have no way of knowing if this present 'arrangement' that you perceive of as your life's history is indeed the result of multitudes of 'successive rolls' or in fact, *just one roll*, a millisecond ago.

On a materialistic account of the world, *everything*, including the thought you are thinking right this very second, reduces to some mass of 'particulates.' As such, though you think you have some memory of past events and believe you are presently experiencing new ones right now (to wit, reading this essay!), your present 'brain state' is in fact indistinguishable from a scenario in which the universe exploded just a second ago, creating in an instant a 'brain state' that was identically configured. By this reasoning one has concluded that all of the reasoning you thought you had done to this point *is as likely* to be an illusion *as it is* to be genuine.

While we presume that the 'arranging' must be orders more complicated and sophisticated than the five dice in our Yahtzee® example, this nonetheless must be true for our present experience of reality on a materialist account. From this it is easy to see that it is fundamentally meaningless to say one knows anything—including that the only thing that exists is the material universe.

Note that on the materialistic outlook, we are precluding the possibility of someone coming along and revealing to us the true situation, as the only entity that could possibly have that information must exist outside the system of 'particulates,' just as the one rolling the dice and the friend who walked in are not themselves, dice.

But it may be objected that the dice do not have a mechanism for recording previous 'brain states' but we have developed mechanistic systems that do have such mechanisms. Turn your attention, they might say, to the computer hard drive.

The hard drive, despite being driven by software, at rock bottom is a series of magnetized sections on a disk that have either a positive or negative charge, which by convention we term either as a '1' or a '0.' By further convention, we can encode information into this 'binary' system, which we can then retrieve later. At first blush, it does seem that the computer has a way to record and recall its own history. Particular configurations of '1s' and '0s' that reflect previous configurations of '1s' and '0s' can be stored almost indefinitely, allowing the computer to refer back to the previous configurations, say, to restore a deleted file or previously visited website. This, then, shows that that information does not need to be seen as immaterial in its essence and furthermore, the material object, the hard drive, is able to tell the difference between past and present.

Further scrutiny, however, shows that the hard drive does not solve the problem, but exacerbates it.

We note in the first place, that this 'information' is of no use or utility to the hard drive itself, and is meaningless without software which is the product of skilled technician and programmers who are third person observers of the hard drive, not the hard drive itself. These people are akin to the ones rolling the dice, with the hard drive now standing in for the dice. However, since on the materialist worldview there is no 'third person' perspective possible, there is no 'skilled technician' or 'programmer' or 'dice roller.' In this analogy, our mind corresponds to the hard drive, not the third person observer. We must consider the hard drive's experience of the world *as a hard drive*.

Now, if the hard drive wishes to entertain the fanciful supposition that it is the product of intelligence which has given its best effort to producing good software and quality components, it may trust to the 'browser history' with some degree of confidence. The various logs containing past updates and the like are probably real and genuine. But what if the hard drive prefers the more sophisticated account, choosing to explain its origin and nature with reference only to the raw 'stuff' of the universe? It thinks it has a case, since it can rightly point to its own base constituents as 'merely' some kind of magnetized (or-demagnetized) material.

But is the hard drive aware of the existence of 'ghosting' programs that can clone the contents of a hard drive *perfectly* and *exactly* to another hard drive? The reader probably knows that data can be backed-up, but the reader may not know that there are programs out there that allow people to make exact duplicates of their hard drives—right down to the 'browser history' and logs containing updates, etc.!

Imagine, if you will, hiring a skilled technician to back-up your complete system while you are enjoying a day on the beach. He performs his task perfectly, right down to using the exact same make, model, and year of the original hard drive. Naturally, you don't take note of the serial number on the respective hard drives, because that is not your concern. When you get home, there on your desk are two completely identical hard drives (excepting, of course, the serial numbers!). But the technician failed to indicate which is the original and which is the copy—probably because he knew very well that it didn't matter.

Like the dice in our previous example, *you* have no way of knowing which hard drive was the result of innumerable 'successive rolls' and which was rolled 'just once.' The die was a six-sided cube with just six options, but the hard drive, as it turns out, is a six-sided cube with many gigabytes of options. Despite the multiplicity of options for the hard drive, in ultimate terms, the exact same problem faces you as you seek to piece out which has the real history and which has the manufactured one.

Now imagine the problem if you are not the one who hired the technician, *but rather the hard drive*.

Any purely mechanistic system can be the result of a single 'toss' or a thousand, or a million. We presume that the brain records data as something other than '1s' and '0s,' but on the materialistic view, it is still just *stuff*.

On the mechanistic view which excludes 'third person revelation' as a possibility, it is impossible for us to know if our ruminations are borne of a lifetime of thoughtful inquiry or a 'toss' of the universe, a mere second ago.

In the face of such realities, many skeptics will simply deride it as inconsequential, since from a pragmatic point of view we must behave as though our perceived 'lifetime' was real or genuine. This view only has merit, however, if one decides to be agnostic. Most materialists prefer to be strident in their outlook, however, and as of this writing, there is a good sized clutch of them who are downright mean in their denigrating of alternative views. They are—coincidentally?—also the ones who are usually the most adamant that mind = brain.

On the above arguments I have maintained that materialism is, in principle, the death of reason itself, and therefore a prime violator of the Golden Rule of Epistemology. The more strident materialists have compounded the matter even further, however, in ways that the unwary may entertain without realizing what is at risk. A quick word needs to be given to these scenarios.

Further Violations of the Golden Rule that Follow from Violating the Golden Rule

Many readers will not be aware of the fact, or have not given enough weight to the fact, that all of the following scenarios are developed from a worldview which explicitly does not allow us to understand reality by reference to a 'third person observer.' To put it bluntly: God is not permitted, in principle, as an explanation. I am not referring to the more benign 'methodological naturalism,' which posits that we should account for the material world without *ad hoc* invocations of a deity, but to a full-blooded 'philosophical naturalism,' which, even if presented with explicit and positive evidence of the deity or its influence, would choose to account for that evidence in naturalistic terms.

To illustrate what I mean, imagine again that you are the hard drive, and you are attempting to make sense of your existence. A great deal can be learned about yourself and your life by examining your constituent parts without positing the existence of a maker. However, if there comes a point where your investigation rationally justifies the inference to a maker, the methodological naturalistic hard drive would be free to do so. The philosophical naturalistic hard drive would not allow itself to contemplate such absurdities, in principle. The reader may judge for himself whether the methodological naturalist hard drive or the philosophical naturalist hard drive is more likely to come to absurd conclusions.

The following scenarios are not the result of methodological naturalistic musing, i.e., empirical investigation, but philosophical naturalistic musing. They pass themselves off as straight-up empirical science when, in fact, they have as their starting point a strict materialism. However, it is precisely because they claim to be the result of empirical inquiry—which any theist or scientist of integrity can welcome—that they become snares to the unwary, drawing right up to the edge of the Golden Rule, and usually lurching like a lemming into the chasm below.

The age and nature of the universe, if conceived in materialistic terms, threaten to violate the Golden Rule. For centuries, there were those who deduced from cause and effect the existence of a First Cause and those who rejected this conclusion, making themselves comfortable with an infinite regress of causes and effects. This basic choice is at the back of many of our arguments today.

An infinite regress of causes and effects is essentially the same as saying that the universe has existed eternally, without beginning and without end. At once we are presented with a difficulty that reminds us of our dice and hard drive, for with an infinite amount of time to 'roll' the particles, it is practically the case that any configuration that is *possible* will at some point be *actual*. You have a 1 in 6 chance of rolling a three on this roll and the next, and the one after that, and a 5 in 6 chance of rolling something else each time, but it is inconceivable, practically speaking, that after a thousand rolls, you will never roll a three. (Try it.)

There is a 1 in x chance of 'rolling' a particular configuration of a hard drive, including one that gives the appearance of a perceived history, but with an infinite amount of time to work with, it will, practically speaking, eventually happen.

There is a 1 in x to the xth chance of 'rolling' a particular configuration of the universe, including one that gives a multitude of hard drives all apparently having the same experience of history, and a multitude of 'brains' likewise experiencing the same history, but given an infinite amount of time to work with, it will eventually happen. How do you know *this* is not *that* moment? *Each* moment?

In materialistic terms, an unending 'universe' means that every possible configuration that is possible, will, at some point, *be*—indeed, it will happen an infinite number of times and be arrived at from an infinite number of routes. You may roll a Yahtzee® by rolling all five dice at once, or by holding on to some in the first and second rolls, improving your odds for the third and final roll. But in this scenario, there are an infinite number of options available, and you will arrive at your Yahtzee® through a variety of ways.

You may be a materialist contemplating this thought and saying, "That's absurd." But that thought is just a configuration of matter which has as much 'meaning' as a five 'threes' comprehending itself. A 'thought' is just the dice, arranged just *so*. For the declaration "that's absurd" to have significance, it must somehow transcend the mere arrangement—it must stand above the arrangement in order to critique it; it must be immaterial in its essence. Just the thing that a materialist won't allow! In short, there is no reason to take such a declaration seriously, and I for one, don't.

But perhaps the materialist objects by pointing out that the universe is not presently understood to be infinite. The so-called 'Big Bang' is said to be the empirically derived theory that the universe is not infinite, but decidedly finite, if very old. But this does not change the materialistic nature of the 'thought' that the universe is finite, if very old. *That* thought itself is just a particular configuration of atoms that we colloquially regard as 'brain state.' We have no way of distinguishing between the 'brain state' where such a 'thought' was 'rolled' a thousand times or just once. It would appear in our 'minds' as exactly the same thing. Our 'empirical' epistemology may have led us to the 'conclusion' that the universe had a finite beginning, but if the epistemology began with the presumption that the only thing that is real is the 'stuff' of the universe, it cannot escape violating the Golden Rule, because its violation was 'baked into the cake.'

The problem is compounded by certain 'discoveries' of the quantum physicists who have shown 'empirically' that reality is itself affected by an observer, such that each time there is an observation, a new universe is created. The so-called 'Multiverse' is a scientifically respected theory of existence that says that there are a near-infinite number of universes parallel to our own where each possible alternative to our own universe is manifested.

The reader is already primed to see how this is a violation of the Golden Rule. If each possible alternative of the universe is manifested, that means every possible materialistic configuration of the universe is actualized 'somewhere,' including the configurations where the configuration occurs in an instant, rather than after billions of supposed years. This 'empirical' line of thought explicitly ends in the conclusion that every possible actuality is actually actualized!

The problem began when the scientists were presented with a genuine empirical mystery, that reality appears to hinge very much on an observer, but the only observers they were willing to consider were part and parcel of the reality under observation; who was observing the observers? Their worldview did not leave room for an Observer; the resulting scenario was absurdity and the death of knowledge and reason itself. We must congratulate them for their genius!

Take for example the "His Dark Material" series by Phillip Pullman which have as their basis a Multiverse scheme. In one universe there is no God (where God is perceived as a temporal being, much as we think of as Zeus, living on a mountain) but he exists in another, where he is a scoundrel (our universe, as it happens.) Pullman is a devout atheist fully aware of the Multiverse and its implications, yet unaware that if the account is right, then even his fictional worlds are real 'somewhere'—and how do we know not this one? He steadfastly mocks the idea of there being a God, but on his understanding of God, there is a universe where he does in fact exist—why not this one? There is a universe where he has looked at the facts of our own present universe and chose instead to be a theist; but facts have nothing to do with making decisions on a materialist view, because that presumes some sort of thought that stands over them the facts to judge between them, but the materialist insists that 'thought' stands shoulder to shoulder with all the other 'brute facts' of our reality.

In other words, even though quantum mechanics was thought to rescue us from determinism, we must conclude that even here everything is determined, or at least, the 'indeterminate' reality is indistinguishable from the determined one: in some universe a person is an atheist and in another a theist, and nothing can be held against either, as if one is more in tune with the 'evidence' than the other. *Every* possibility *will be* manifested. There is also a universe where Pullman wakes up one morning thinking he is a muddled mass of puss and rock, and he would be quite right—just as right as he is today in his conclusion that he is an atheist, and just as right as I am today in my conclusion that I am a theist.

If the reader perceives that this is a violation of the law of the excluded middle and hence the death of logic and hence

18

(if true), the death of any ability to ascertain truth about the world in any intelligible fashion, i.e., a violation of the Golden Rule of Epistemology, then you've grasped the problem. But that is strict materialism for you.

Remember, on this view, even the idea of 'right' must somehow consist of a pattern of atoms. It just so happens we ascribe a kind of value to this particular pattern. But even the idea of 'value' and the 'act of ascribing' is a particular pattern of atoms, and so too the idea of 'idea.'

But Natural Selection Rescues us From Chance!

But the materialist has another ace up his sleeve.

Remember the rabid evolutionist and 'new atheist' Richard Dawkins, who boldly declared in his book, *The Blind Watchmaker*, that thanks to Darwin, it was possible to be an intellectually satisfied atheist. The problem Dawkins wishes to attack in this book is the argument from design. Biology gives every appearance of design (indeed, Dawkins says it is much more pronounced than proponents of design themselves realize), which was *prima facie* evidence for a designer. For the honest 'methodological naturalist,' something that is *apparently* designed is *prima facie* evidence of it being *actually* designed. For the philosophical naturalist, however, all apparent design must be only that— *apparently* designed. (The argument, of course, is never extended to the things that we humans design! Only the things that exhibit orders more sophistication that go beyond all human capabilities and conception in their appearance of design are singled out as 'apparently designed.') How this could possibly be the case, however, was the weak underbelly of the atheistic argument for thousands of years. Until Darwin.

Contrary to what many people believe, Darwinism, as Darwin himself advanced it, is not compatible with theism. Darwin specifically sought out to explain all organisms on the planet without reference to a deity. This was one of his stated goals. His program, therefore, was to find a purely materialistic way to account for everything, including humans, and including the human mind—which, on his view, must only be 'brain.'

Many people, including many theists, have attempted to reconcile themselves with Darwinism, either unaware of, or uncaring about, the strictly materialistic starting point that Darwin himself adopted. This is unwise on a number of levels. It would be as if someone said, "Let us assume that there is no God; therefore, there is no God" and the other fellow, a theist, said, sincerely, "Ah, that is some mighty fine thinking there. Your argument is stronger than I supposed! But I will remain a theist."

If it surprises the theist that he has not won the respect of evolutionists in that case, it shouldn't surprise anyone else. The evolutionist is quite right in wondering why the belief in the deity persists, when the whole argument dispenses with that belief.[3] The better approach would be to challenge the initial assumption, and then see what kind of evolutionary account might merit our attention and respect.

But back to Darwin and his attempt to account for life on this planet in purely mechanistic terms.

His solution was to assert that the organisms of this planet could be explained by the simple processes of elimination and reproduction and that the evidence supported this explanation. Those organisms that survived to reproduce would come to populate the world, while those that for some reason could not survive and reproduce would not. Their descendents would be subjected to the same pressures. One thing led to another, and here we are.

These 'simple processes of elimination' are termed 'selection.' The organisms that remain after the elimination are presumed to be better suited for survival in their

---

[3] For example, Francis Collins is a Christian who fully accepts Darwinism, but Richard Dawkins and Daniel Dennett still hold him in contempt.

environment, and are said to have 'adapted' to it. Since 'selection' and 'adaptation' are in play, the Darwinian account is supposed to be excluded from the game of 'chance.' This is sleight of hand; both the phrases 'selection' and 'adaptation' carry with them the sense of conscious, intelligent agents *selecting* and *adapting.* Describing mindless mechanisms in terms that connote deliberate choosing makes for good self-serving propaganda, but it doesn't change the underlying fact that what you are describing is chock full of chance.

After all, if a meteor crashes into a flock of sheep, it doesn't follow that the ones that survived have 'adapted' themselves to crashing meteors. It just means that they were lucky enough not to be struck by the meteor. But the problem runs deeper than that. In order for actual changes to occur in later populations, there have to be mutations in the genetic code. Supposing that in our flock of sheep there were specimens with an advantage against meteor strikes (with some, perhaps, having bony, fireproof shields on their backs), the advantage must have been developed before the threat manifested—obviously, or else the sheep wouldn't have survived to reproduce. Since there is no 'mind' to predict the arrival of a meteor, and no 'mind' to tweak the DNA of the sheep in light of the coming threat, the fact that they *happened* to have the necessary mutations at the right time and place can only be a matter of blind luck.

We do not need to delve deeper into what is empirically known about how genetic mutations actually occur (unpredictably, and *almost always* deleteriously; i.e., more *chance*) in order to recognize that on this view they cannot happen in anticipation of, and in preparation for, a specific threat. For, 'anticipation' and 'preparation' are like the terms 'selection' and 'adaptation' in that they necessarily imply some kind of intelligent agency, which the Darwinian viewpoint purposefully excludes as one of its first principles. Since conscious purpose is not on the table, we have to conclude that the fact that this particular population of sheep happened to have some among them with bony backs prior to the arrival of the meteor is a matter of sheer luck.[4]

Unfortunately, meteor strikes and other natural phenomena are not *themselves* subjected to natural selection. Even if we allowed that natural selection could rise above the charge of chance, 'acts of God,' which must have occurred and been factors countless times over the distant ages, would remain in the realm of odds and probabilities.

The Darwinian defense to this is that the 'process of elimination' is not arbitrary, because there is a rhyme and reason for why some organisms might live or die, but as illustrated, just because a process is not arbitrary, it is not immune from chance. It is likewise not arbitrary that in a game of Yahtzee® only the numbers of one through six will turn up on the roll of a die, but it remains a matter of chance which of the six will turn up. It remains a matter of chance that the 'meteor strike' has need of a pair of two's, and thus eliminates all of the four's and five's, leaving only the two's to 'survive.'

One response that I've heard to this line of argument is that, while we don't know and can't know all of the details of how we got here, we do observe natural selection at work, and well, here we are! Which is to say, we have no other way to explain biology in completely naturalistic terms except for natural selection, so however it happened to work, it *did* happen. The fact that we are 'here' is proof enough. God, as you recall, is not even allowed on the table as a possible explanation. If you push hard enough on any atheist's argument, this is where you arrive, and if you think that this sounds awfully a lot like 'faith' just don't tell them that. They are likely to have an aneurism.

However, you can avoid causing their untimely death by pointing out that, on this development of their view, the

---

[4] I must regret to inform the reader, however, that there was such a population of bony-backed sheep who were fortunate enough to be so prepared. However, as fate would have it, the meteor scored a direct hit on them, and they all died.

epistemological challenge to epistemology only compounds itself. On top of the intrinsic problem posed by a materialistic fabric of the universe, and the necessity of invoking countless fortuitous events (within the genome and within geo-physics, etc), the alleged success of our non-arbitrary, but lucky, arrival in the universe brings with it yet more violations of the Golden Rule.

The Information Fly in the Ointment

Recall that on the Darwinian viewpoint, transgression of the Golden Rule is supposed to be avoided because the organisms 'selected' must, by virtue of its structure (including its 'brain states'), conform better to reality the way reality really is than ones that do not, or else it could not survive, let alone reproduce. Unfortunately, *the very most* that Darwinism can say about a given organism's 'conforming to reality' is that it is *enough* to survive to reproduction.

It is entirely conceivable that an organism has an entirely false, illusory, or just incomplete conception of reality, that nonetheless allows it to survive to reproduce. For example, a creature about to eat something that is toxic to him, and will kill him, may just as easily choose not to because "it smells terrible" as having the thought, "it killed my two friends who I just watched eat it" as having the thought, "that substance is poisonous" as having the thought, "that is cyanide." There are a variety of conceivable mechanisms by which a 'brain state' could warn an organism against a substance that would kill it, and it is not by any means certain that this would happen before or after it reproduced. One may indeed suppose that certain organisms were the ones left after the 'poison' did its worst—akin to what we hear about bacterial resistance to antibiotics. No one supposes the bacteria that are left have somehow 'learned' anything. They survived an otherwise hostile environment, that is all.

We trust that our senses give us good information about the true nature of the world, but in fact, all we really 'know' is that the information is 'good enough' that we are generally able to survive and reproduce. There could be—nay, there *must be*—any number of aspects of reality that are foreclosed to us that we cannot directly sense. For example, we cannot make our way through the world via echolocation like a bat does. It literally experiences the world in a way that we can only approximate, and we can never know how close our approximation really is. Similarly, a bat may have a more heightened appreciation for the true nature of a giant object, say, thirty foot wide by fifteen foot tall; but apparently, it is unable to sense or decode the information that we have put on that object which we, by convention, call a billboard.

For all we know, there is information encoded all around us of a similar sort, but just as the bat's echolocation is able to perceive the aspect of reality that manifests as words and pictures on the billboard, we are unable to perceive the aspects of reality that manifest in our environment, which our senses have not evolved to detect, since our survival and reproduction were not impacted by them. A bat does not need to know what product is being sold on the billboard, it only needs to know it is there, and swerve away. There could be far more to a 'tree' than we perceive; we only need to know it is there to not run into it. For all we know, a bat perceives the real nature of a tree better than we do.

I have made reference to the possibility of there being more 'information' around us, pointing out the bat's superior ability to navigate space, but its inability to detect information encoded into that space, but there is much more to peel back behind the phrase, "trust that our senses give us good information about the true nature of the world." The fact that our senses *give us information* is itself necessary to examine from this point of view.

Take, for example, the so-called 'light sensitive spot' that is supposed (as Rudyard Kipling supposes things) to have led to the development of eyesight. On this view, we can relatively easily see organisms—or even compounds—that change on account of light and heat, and this on an entirely mechanistic scheme. We are to imagine that the light that reaches our brains is similarly mechanistic, as if a photon hits this spot in our eyeball which trips a pulley which yanks a lever which presses a button which gives us an 'image.' On this view, it is just a series of material objects that are cobbled together, and it is not hard to imagine, given enough time, and exposed to heat and the right conditions, for 'stuff' to assort themselves into a pattern.

The reader may already have winced at the thought of all this stuff being 'cobbled together' and wondering with me just how well we could trust such a process in regards to epistemology. The appeal to great time, which is supposed to be the savior of evolutionary schemes, actually creates further pangs of doubt, since if one is to believe that 'enough time and the right conditions' could produce *this* result, it could, *and would*, create *that* result, where *that* result might *just as likely* be that our whole universe was thrown together a second ago, giving the appearance that we evolved. Only now, it is the evolutionist himself opening the door to that likelihood, since it is he that is invoking the mysterious powers of infinite time in order to rescue his extremely precarious position.[5]

Stating this basic flaw in the materialistic outlook is now

---

[5] Which heretofore he had insisted was based squarely on *science*. We were mercilessly bullied into believing that this viewpoint rests on rock-solid empirical evidence, but if we punch the bully in the nose we discover his argument consists actually of a philosophical 'Hail Mary.' Remember that in the game of American football, the opponent is *just as likely* to catch the football in the end zone as your own team. So, if we use 'great time' to make it more plausible that natural processes could create humans in all their glory over the millennia, the plausibility that we were created by natural processes in an instant, with the appearance of having arisen over the millennia, is also increased. The reason why the atheists are bullies on this point is because they wish to improve their chances that their 'Hail Mary' will work by shoving their opponents off the field altogether. This has been a successful tactic, but it will cease being successful by standing up to the bullies. Also, just pointing out that their argument only 'works' *because* they are bullies you can persuade people of integrity to look upon their argument more critically.

becoming redundant, but in this context we have to mention it again because in this instance the 'answer' to this charge actually *compounds* the difficulties radically, because it *is not* the case that what we perceive as an 'image' is the result of mechanistic objects banging around in reaction to photons. Instead, we know that light is converted *into information* which the brain then processes into a representation. We *never* directly apprehend things by sight.

This is one of the very difficulties philosophers have grappled with in trying to describe just what 'reality' really is. What we perceive is something that is within our mind, not the thing itself. It may be that we cannot avoid living as though the world exists independently of our trajectory through it, but we have *just as much* grounds—if we exclude the help of other minds—as concluding that the world exists solely and wholly within our skulls as representations made by 'brain states.' But all of this rumination presumes that the information processing going on in our skulls is 'working.'

To put it another way, consider again our hard drive. As it sits there, it cannot know anything about the world. The best it can do is think about its own internal self. This can be remedied by supplying to it data about the world around it. Devices that detect audio and visual cues from the world can be made that can provide that data. However, heat, sound, and light, are not directly transmitted to the hard drive for consideration. It is converted into 'ones' and 'zeros'... by software. Moreover, in order for the hard drive to ascribe any significance to this stream of 'ones' and 'zeros,' it needs an 'operating system.' More software.

Insofar as the hard drive can trust to the careful work of intelligent agents, it can rely on the software to tell it the truth about external reality. But what if the hard drive decides that since the information is encoded into 'ones' and 'zeros' just like anything else it apprehends, that is all information *is*, can it still rely on the software? Of course, for the hard drive to 'decide' anything, requires trusting the software!

The Darwinian approach requires us to suppose that millions of years of unguided processes produced not just the bio-mechanical systems, but 'software' that accurately converts the data into some other form which is then processed with fidelity and represented within our skulls as genuine reflections of what is actually going on in the world outside our skulls.

To make matters worse (if it could get any worse), Darwin could get along hoping that morphological changes could happen mechanistically, as if the building blocks of life were akin to those wooden toy blocks that many children grew up with. Given enough time and the filter of reality, it seems plausible that one could randomly shake those blocks and have it result in, say, the shape of a kitchen table. With more shaking, and enough time, it seems plausible that the blocks for the 'legs' of the table and the surface of it might be retained, and a back added to it so that now, without appeal to a designer, get the shape of a kitchen chair. Darwin could conceive of morphological change like this because he was wholly unaware of DNA.

But morphological changes are actually the result of information encoded into our cells. You can get no change at all by shaking the 'blocks' around because the structure is the function of something like a blueprint. If you cut off a man's arm, his child will not be born without an arm, because we do not get new morphological structures by shaking bits of body parts around, but through a combining of information from the blueprint supplied by a man and the blueprint supplied by the woman, to create a blueprint for the new human.

To return to our toy block analogy and try to imagine it along the lines that biological change actually happens, it would not be the case that the new forms occur by shaking the blocks into new patterns, but by adjusting a blueprint, which then results in a new pattern. This is precisely what happens when a two year old dismantles the kitchen table it made and creates instead a kitchen chair, only the blueprint is not committed to paper, but resides in the mind of that two year old. In short, for morphological change to occur in biological systems, it must happen *first at the level of the blueprint*.

One does not get from a 'light sensitive spot' to the human eyeball by moving bits of 'blocks' around. It would require progressive changes of the DNA itself at each step, miraculously holding onto the pieces of information that gave rise to an arrangement that allowed the organism to survive to reproduce while producing—not new morphological arrangements, but *new DNA arrangements* that produced new morphological arrangements—that gradually produced a nervous system that integrated into a mass of brain cells that could process convert the light into information and recombine it into a representation that correlates to reality.

To make matters worse—*as if it could get any worse!*— we have five senses, not just one! This same problem applies to all of our senses, not just our eyesight. One hears endlessly about 'light sensitive spots' because no one has yet contrived of 'sound sensitive' or 'scent sensitive' or 'touch sensitive' or 'taste sensitive' spots.

In all these cases, it is not some raw brute facts of reality banging into other raw brute facts that we are talking about (i.e., light hitting a 'spot' that happens to be sensitive to being hit) but rather the converting of that event into a data stream which is then converted into a representation which we believe corresponds to reality *as it really is*.

The doubt that this casts upon our confidence that we really do perceive reality as it really is must be immediate to anyone who has ever actually thought about it. (Darwinians usually don't. That's why they are Darwinians.) To account for all of these components—the light and sound, etc... the morphological structures themselves... the DNA encoding and the changing of that DNA encoding over time... the conversion of brute facts into information... the transmission of that information into the brain... the processing of that information... the representation this processing generates and our apprehension of that representation as correlating to reality—a process called natural selection is invoked.

But remember the bat. On top of all of the above, we now have to add in the fact that we must acknowledge that there are more 'senses' that we lack, and thus more to reality than we realize. We not only have to suppose that our current senses yield good information that corresponds to reality but that it is sufficient to make generalizations about reality. We do not know what we do not know. Why these senses and not some other senses? Why not some senses and not all of them?

The only answer Darwinism allows is that the ones we have are ones that permitted us to survive to reproduction. There is no warrant beyond that threshold of accuracy. The best that the formula "survive to reproduce" can obtain is some *approximation* to reality, but we can never, *in principle*, know just how good of an approximation our apprehension of the world is. We act as though it is 99% close, when throughout the animal kingdom there are organisms that we believe have 1% or less comprehension of the world. They seem to get along just fine with their (we think) inferior grasp of reality. On the same principle, maybe it is *we* that have 1% or less comprehension of the world, and by comparison these other organisms have a tiny fraction of that one percent. *How do we know* this isn't the case, and it just so happens our grasp is sufficient *only to the extent* that we can survive and reproduce, too?

Because of *our brain*? But the 'brain' is itself the result of the same selection pressures, and plenty of other 'brains' in the animal kingdom seem to survive to reproduction without recourse to what we call 'reason.' Or so we think.

Darwinism, on its own terms, is unable to give any assurance that we have a grasp of reality above and beyond what is necessary to survive and reproduce. As such, far from upholding the Golden Rule of Epistemology, Darwinian evolution veers wildly into transgressing it.

Indeed, it utterly and completely demolishes even the pretense that we really know anything. It isn't even that it takes epistemology for granted, but, like the Multiverse, explicitly demands that we take our reasoning as an illusion of some sort. Our awareness of an 'abstraction' such as the 'law of non-contradiction' is just as easily a mechanism that can be isolated within our 'brains' like we think we identify genes in our DNA, that happens to keep us from thinking that we can having our cake and eat it too—perhaps, in reality as it really is, that sort of thing happens all the time! Perhaps in another universe.

Thus, if Darwinism is true, there is no way to know it.

Does Pragmatism Trump Logic?

In a last ditch effort to salvage the position, the atheist may say, "Ah, but we cannot actually live that way!" To which I can plaintively retort, "Which is precisely all we could hope for from a process that is geared only to 'creating' organisms that survive to reproduction."

A good illustration of this and much of what I've written so far is found in something that Edward Slingerland wrote in *Creating Consilience*. Emphasis in the original, as he writes:

> ...from the perspective of evolutionary psychology, I can be convinced on an intellectual level that the love that I feel toward my child and my relatives is an emotion installed in me by my genes in accordance with Hamilton's Rule. This does not, however, make my visceral, "on-line" experience of the emotion, nor my sense of its normative reality, any less real to me. At an important and ineradicable level, the idea of my daughter as merely a complex robot carrying my genes into the next generation is both bizarre and repugnant to me. Indeed, this is precisely what one would expect according to evolutionary theory: Gene-level, ultimate causation

would not work unless we were thoroughly sincere at the proximate level. The whole purpose of the evolution of social emotions is to make sure that these "false" feelings seem inescapably real to us, and this lived reality will never change unless we turn into completely different organisms. In a similar way we can say, qua physicalists, that our overactive theory of mind causes us to inevitably project intentionality onto the world—to see our moral emotions and desires writ large in the cosmos, or to see some sort of "meaning" in our lives. It would, moreover, be empirically unjustified to take this projection as "real." Nonetheless, the very inevitably of this projection means that, whatever we may assert as physicalists, we cannot escape from the lived reality of moral space. As neuroscientists, we might believe that the brain is a deterministic, physical system like everything else in the universe, and recognize that the weight of empirical evidence suggests that free will is a cognitive illusion. Nonetheless, no cognitively undamaged human being can help *acting* like and at some level really *feeling* that he or she is free. There may well be individuals who lack this sense, and who can quite easily and thoroughly conceive of themselves and other people in purely instrumental, mechanistic terms, but we label such people "psychopaths," and quite rightly try to identify them and put them away somewhere to protect the rest of us. The Darwinian model of the origin of human beings and other animals, and its formulation of the ultimate reasons for many of our abilities and behaviors, is thus theoretically powerful and satisfying while appearing alien, and often repugnant, from any normal human perspective.

So there you have it. If you accept the Darwinian account *and really live that way*, you are a psychopath who should be locked up. *His* words! He would have us believe that we should accept the Darwinian account intellectually, but live as though it were not true, all the while acknowledging that our experience of reality is "false." But it is our experience of reality that is said to tell us, intellectually, that Darwinism is correct![6]

What if We Introduce Intelligence to Darwinian Processes?

Conceivably, dispensing with the atheistic underpinning and replacing it with a theistic one, an evolutionary theory could be redeemed. If there was an intelligent agent involved over these long years, carefully tinkering with our nervous systems and 'software,' some confidence in our epistemology could be restored.

Unfortunately, most people who turn to a Darwinian scheme do so precisely because of its perceived support for an atheistic worldview, and have no desire to introduce theism at the last moment, invoking 'special creation' at the end when they denounced it at the beginning. After all, while it is theoretically possible to talk about intelligent agents with the ability to generate the biological sophistication we observe, everyone understands that the best candidate, obviously, is God.

Still, you will still hear ideas such as 'directed panspermia' floated in response to such arguments, in particular to 'abiogenesis,' since no one has yet managed to conceive of a way that life got started in the first place. Darwinian processes are supposed to 'kick in' once the biological system is established, but few, if anyone, thinks

---

[6] This framework can only be "theoretically powerful and satisfying" if one is tremendously motivated to exclude God as an explanation. He tips his hand to this effect by stating plainly that our "theory of mind ... inevitably" creates the illusion of higher thought at work in the universe and our own sense of "meaning." In other words, in our daily life it is natural, normal, expected, *and sane*, that we live *as though* there really is a God. It would *be insane* to actually live as though there were not a God. But there isn't a God. *See?*

that Darwinian processes could have themselves established the system. Thus, hyper-intelligent space aliens 'planting' life on the earth is one idea that has been proposed. Seriously. Children are able to spot the next obvious question: "Where did the hyper-intelligent space aliens come from?"

Evidently, these space aliens are themselves the result of Darwinian processes, but note that on this view, the 'great time' that was previously allocated to making our own origin and development plausible now must be invoked to account for the space aliens. If we get 5 billion years, then they also ought to get 5 billion years. But we might say, perhaps the hyper-intelligent space aliens were themselves planted by hyper-hyper-intelligent space aliens. Hard to imagine, right? But not if we allow them 5 billion years to develop, too! But now we are back to the very origins of the universe, and we haven't billions of years to spare.

If the reader is having great fun engaging in such imaginative and speculative theorizing, you may further commend yourself, since you are engaging in what in these latter days has become considered rock-solid scientific investigation.

GIGO

I think it says something about the state of mind of those who uphold an atheistic evolutionary viewpoint that we are led to believe our choice is between the machinations of mindless nature working itself out over the eons or an intelligence that is beyond our comprehension, as the systems we are discussing are orders more complicated and intricate than any that humans have concocted or every hope to concoct. A single human brain is more wondrous than all of the computers of the world, *combined.* Yet no one doubts that computers are the product of intelligent design, but many earnestly put forward the notion that our human brains definitely aren't.

Darwinian accounts do not escape the more basic fact that

atheism is intrinsically in violation of the Golden Rule of Epistemology. An atheistic evolutionary paradigm kills the reasonableness of reason twice-over, first by axiom and second by conclusion; GIGO, as they say. We must now make it clear that the evolutionary aspect is not the part that deals the deathblow to epistemology, for, as just mentioned, a reference to an intelligent agent could resolve that part. The real problem is entertaining a scenario where that agent exists at our own plane of existence: a more superior 'hard drive' than the hard drive we are used to, or a more sophisticated collection of dice than our five dice. (Ie., hyper-hyper-intelligent space aliens.)

If the universe itself could regard itself, instead of entities within it regarding it,[7] it would still be unable to determine if it had a genuine history or appeared in an instant, and it could not know if its knowledge was true.

So we arrive at a point where we must conclude that for epistemology, for reason, for logic, for our comprehension of 'reality' as we think 'it really is,' we cannot entertain explanations that consist solely of factors within our own frame of reference. We must either appeal to a 'third person perspective' or cease being thinkers at all. That is, embrace the world only as animals—eating, drinking, and making merry. There can only be rational thought *at all* if there is a

---

[7] Some versions of pantheism regard the universe itself as sentient and self-aware. Atheists tend to think of pantheists as being as nutty as theists, but if we consider ourselves sentient and self-aware, and we are wholly contained within the universe, and composed only of universal 'stuff,' couldn't we argue that at the very least, the universe does regard itself—through us! More broadly, the idea that the universe has a mind tends to be ridiculed by those who believe we are the result of utterly mindless processes, which leads to the head-scratching proposal that humans exhibit a capacity that the universe does not have. How can humans express something that the universe itself cannot? Atheists try to head off this reasoning by pointing to 'emergent' realities, where the whole is greater, and qualitatively different, than the parts. In other words, an emergent reality is a transcendental one... except it isn't, because that would render their worldview null and void.

Rational Thinker, and this Thinker cannot be part and parcel of our own level of existence.

And this raises a number of reasonable questions the minute we think the thought.

PROVED: Man Does Not Exist!

One of the first reasonable questions was famously put by Euthyphro: is God good because goodness transcends him and he must obey it? If so, he is not the highest being, i.e., not God. Or, is 'good' just whatever God declares? If so, then 'goodness' is the result of capricious whim and arbitrary declaration—not the sort of being we should give our honor and allegiance to. After all, God could just as easily declare that we ought to murder six million people in ovens, and we would have to regard that as 'good.' If 'God' tells us to be 'good' by not stealing, murdering, or (the real concern of most people looking to escape a God-dictated morality) committing adultery, we shouldn't give it much weight. These are just arbitrary judgments he has made that he could just as easily reverse.

Euthyphro raised this as an argument against the existence of God, for it seemed to him that the matter was intractable. He would have it instead that morality and 'goodness' be recognized as a social convention which a society could alter and mold as it desired. Therein we see the problem: Euthyphro has not resolved the problem, but moved it. Instead of being applied to God, the problem now resides atop society, or any given individual. Are we not right, then, in asking, "is something good inherently, which we must obey? If so, then there is something higher than us, and we are not gods. But if 'good' is whatever we decide is 'good' it is not the sort of thing to get all bent out of shape about; eat, drink, and be merry—slaughter your fellow man and rape his wife, if you like. Or not, as you please (because your fellow man might try to rape *your* wife.)"

Since the dilemma applies as equally to man as it does to God, then it must follow that just as there is no God, there is no man! *Waitaminute...*

Ok, Then Maybe... A Prime *Everything*

But if the Euthyphro Dilemma is weak at the knees, it still conjures up a deep and enduring mystery. A classical argument for theism is that of the 'prime mover.' An infinite regress of causes and effect is deemed logically untenable, leading to the deduction of a causeless causer. In the case of morality, we appear to be faced with a similar progression. The difference is only that no one imagined that man could possibly be a candidate for the 'causeless causer' but it didn't seem self-evidently absurd that man could be the 'moral moralizer.' But *it is* absurd.

The escape from Euthyphro's dilemma is to understand that the matter is mysterious, and must always be so, but that in order for logic and reason to prevail, in areas of morality, we must infer the existence of a Prime Moralizer.

Now we discover a profound truth. It is not just 'cause and effect' that forces us to infer the existence of a 'prime' entity. Morality does so as well. But there are others: Logic and human rationality has driven us to infer the existence of a Prime Thinker. Our inability to peel back language itself to directly apprehend truth suggests the existence of a Prime Communicator. Schroedinger's Cat led the quantum theorists to posit countless universes to accommodate all of the outcomes generated by near-infinite observations because the idea of a Prime Observer was forbidden. In order to know that our past experiences are real and genuine, and not made in an instant, there is need for a Prime Dice-Thrower and Prime Computer Technician. In order for us to consider our experience of reality in any coherent, reasonable fashion, at every turn we are compelled to accept the existence of *the Prime*.

And whatever the Prime may be, it cannot be the same as us or coterminous with the universe—if we wish to maintain that reason is reasonable. Whatever the Prime may be, it must be above and beyond it, and strikingly, Other.

Historically and conventionally, we call this Other, God.

Our choice is basic: reject the existence of God, and abandon any reasonable basis for trusting in our reasoning at all, or accept the existence of God, allowing all 'regresses' to resolve finally in Him.

PART THREE: HOW CHRISTIAN THEISM COHERES WITH THE RULE

I could leave the argument here, but it leaves many questions unanswered. Many proposals have been put forward as to the nature of *the Prime*, and if we acknowledged that many of them have been mutually exclusive, that would be to put it mildly. Convincing people that God exists is an important part of my life's program, but helping them to understand the way that Christianity has historically conceived of Him tends to be an emphasis, because many people do not reject Christianity, but some package of notions they mistake for Christianity. Furthermore, if Christianity is correct, it is not enough to know that there is a God, or even that he is as Christianity conceives him, for, according to the Christian writer, James, even the demons know *that*—and tremble.

Nonetheless, I don't think it would be prudent to take this essay that far. Instead, I think it better for present purposes to show how Christianity uniquely handles some of the concerns raised above. I wish to show how Christianity's God is a superior candidate for the Prime. It is up to the reader to proceed from there, although if they wish to contact me for further 'connecting of the dots' I'd be happy to do my best.

Can the Prime 'Other' Communicate?

The conclusion that there is a Prime Mover was reached by Aristotle, without any reference to Christian theology. He proceeded to make a series of deductions from this same line of argument, and many of them weren't consistent with

Christian theology. There is an important distinction to be made in our epistemology: there are some things we can know by direct inspection, but others that we know, and sometimes can only be known, by the revelation of others. Aristotle did his best with 'unaided' inquiry into the nature of the Other, but it goes without saying that the best source of information on the nature and intent and will of the Other is the Other Himself.

To put it bluntly, Aristotle had no access to revelation.

The reader would be mistaken if he saw this as some kind of cop-out, since the reader relies on revelation all of the time. The reader would know nothing about Leonardo Da Vinci without revelation, for the reader was not alive to directly apprehend the man. One must go to the records left by the man and by those who knew him. The same is true of almost everything we know about historical events and purposes.

Even that which we think we know about the laws of nature through the methodology of science comes to us by revelation. Not one of us—including any scientists who may be reading this—have carried out even 1% of the experiments that have been conducted over the centuries. Have you, dear reader, measured for yourself the speed of light? Have you excluded the existence of the ether by your own empirical analysis? Have you experimented with magnetism, alloys, and motion, in order to learn for yourself the things that you think are true?

No. The vast majority of the things you think are true were revealed to you by others, and for various reasons you decided these people were reliable revealers of that information. They were your parents, or your teachers, or your peers. Not only is there nothing inherently suspicious about 'revelation' as an epistemological method, a vast majority of what we 'know' is acquired that way.

But we have inferred the existence of something that is 'outside' or 'beyond' our plane of existence. We had to do this in order to place our own reason on a reasonable basis, but except for some telling clues here and there (and they *are* telling clues), we know little about the character and personality of this 'something.'

For example, we may come into a room and find an empty gallon of chocolate ice cream, and this would allow us to reasonably infer the existence of an eater of that ice cream. But, does it follow that the eater *liked* the chocolate ice cream? Perhaps the eater was made to do so at gun point. Perhaps the eater likes other ice cream more, but it was not available. Does the eater also enjoy watching reruns of the television show, "Cheers"? Merely inferring the existence of someone or something leaves many questions unanswered and unanswerable. Much comes clear if the eater comes into the room to explain himself.

But this is not strictly possible for the Other. In order for God to make himself known to us, he cannot do it as God, but as some form of the 'stuff' we are familiar with, arranged in such a way as to convey the message he wishes to convey. But how to distinguish this 'message' from the 'stuff,' and moreover, as a 'message' from the Other?

Theorists have been tackling the former question for a long time, but not theologically; rather they have wrestled with how *all* agents communicate with each other. This is important to note, because the notion of 'revelation' is commonly ridiculed by those who reject the existence of God, as though the problems associated with discerning that revelation and testing its veracity are substantially different than the problems we humans have even when communicating with each other.

'Communication' is essentially the same as 'revelation.' The difference is that communication presupposes a mutual sharing of information, whereas 'revelation' may be uni-directional. Where it is at least bi-directional, we call it 'communication.'

The advent of computers brought with it the need for finding a way to have them communicate, and then to encode within that framework our own communications, with the computer, and with ourselves. This required hard work and hard thinking, but it wasn't insurmountable, and despite exploitations of weaknesses intrinsic to the medium (i.e., the possibility of 'phishing', where someone pretends to be another person for purposes of stealing personal information), in the main, we've made it work.

But that was human-to-human communication. It has intrinsic difficulties, but it doesn't follow that just because there are such difficulties, communication (i.e., 'revelation') is impossible or absurd or that the communicators themselves do not exist! People misunderstand each other all the time, but no one concludes that because there is a misunderstanding, the other person must not exist!

There are intrinsic difficulties facing God if he wishes to communicate with us and before we dismiss the notion of Revelation as absurd on its face, we must take these into account. Rest assured, God would be aware of them, even if we were not!

We must keep constantly in mind what relation our universe must have to God.

Transcendence *required...*

Since we have concluded that God is Prime, and not the universe, it must follow that the universe is wholly contingent. God must exist 'outside' of the universe in some fashion that we find difficult to fathom. Since God is the only non-contingent thing, the universe, as contingent, must be contained *within* God, for if the universe existed somehow outside of God, the universe would be as Prime as God is—rendering *neither* of them as Prime, *by definition.* This 'outsideness' we call 'transcendence.'

The fact that God transcends our reality is imperative to keep in mind. Atheists such as Richard Dawkins and Philip Pullman (and 'new' atheists in general) think of God as a local, temporal being, which could possibly be detected by pointing a telescope in the right direction or climbing the right mountain.[8] The Prime could never be detected in that way, by the very definition of the Prime.

And Immanence, too

But there is another implication flowing from our recognition that the universe is wholly contingent. We said that it must be contained *within* God somehow, because if it wasn't, we'd have to acknowledge the existence of some other kind of non-contingent plane of existence, where the universe could stand separate and distinct from God. This necessarily required us to acknowledge that God *transcends* the universe, but it also requires us to acknowledge that God is wholly *immanent* within our universe.

You must fix in your mind what we are talking about here. We ruled out the possibility of an actual infinite regression on a number of levels—cause and effect, reasonableness of reason, morality, observation, etc.—forcing us to admit the existence of something that is the First Cause, the First Reasoner, the First Moralizer, the First Observer, and so-on. This 'First' entity must be of an entirely different nature than all that followed. It must be the whole sum of all that there is; there can only be one non-contingent 'thing,' which in turn must be categorically different than all that follows, which is contingent. This 'sum

---

[8] Think: Zeus. 'New Atheists' constantly invoke such entities, often in the context of making some form of the argument "we are both atheists, I just believe in one less god than you." This shows a thoroughly flawed comprehension of Christian theology, and even basic literacy. They founder on the fact that Zeus is called 'a god' while Christians talk about God, as though 'God' and 'a god' are categorically the same kind of thing. No matter how much one explains the difference, it has no impact on their understanding of the situation; this is one of the distinguishing traits of a 'New Atheist.' A much better comparison to the Christian God than Zeus would be the Demiurge. This author has never once seen a 'New Atheist' mention the Demiurge. It is hard to believe that the 'New Atheists' are unaware of the Demiurge. Their insistence on using Zeus-like characters rather than the Demiurge is probably because their argument is based on ridicule, not reason, and Zeus, they feel, is more likely to inspire others to find theism as ridiculous as *they* do.

of all there is' we are calling 'God.'

That means that there is nowhere that one can go to escape the knowledge and power of God. It is not possible to exist except by the working, somehow, of this God, and that goes for all of our constituent parts, and all parts of the universe. Each atom or subatomic particle of the universe must be fully known to God and must somehow be tied intimately to his being. And yet, it cannot in any respect be identified *as* Him.

Richard Dawkins, in his *Delusion*, scoffs about the 'mind-reading' abilities of the local deity, 'Yahweh,' not realizing that by the definition of the thing in view, it is not possible for the Prime to *not* know our thoughts, or anything else in existence, for if anything was not directly knowable to the Prime, the Prime would not be the Prime.

These two aspects of the Prime have been known to humanity for eons. The pantheists, of course, considered the universe the 'sum of all that there is' and felt that there had to be some intelligence to it. Theirs was a conception of God that was immanent, certainly, because God and the universe were the same thing. Deists, on the other hand, conceive of a transcendent being, but understand him to be a distant entity that started up the universe and then stepped away; but that entails the idea that it is even possible for the universe to exist on its own power or plane of existence, apart from God.

Reason demands us to reject both of those conceptions and look for about for a description of the Prime that incorporates his transcendent nature and his immanent nature.

Christianity Delivers

Christianity does just this. The clearest passage is found in Ephesians 4:

"There is one body and one Spirit [...] one Lord, one faith, one baptism; one God and Father of all, who is *over* all and *through* all and *in* all." [italics added]

Here you have the 'Primeness' and its transcendence and immanence plainly stated.[9]

Christianity's Take on How the Prime Communicates With Us

Now, just *how* does a non-contingent entity like God communicate to contingent entities swimming in a contingent medium, which we call the 'universe'? *How* can we distinguish those communications from communications originating by other entities within that medium? After all, the communications will have to be transmitted to us through the exact same mechanisms, means, and modes that we receive communications from our fellow contingent entities, and the philosophers already know how problematic that is!

I would guess that there are two answers that come instinctively to mind.

In the first place, the premise of the question might be rejected by insisting that God is not at all limited to the 'exact same mechanisms, means, and modes' of communication we are already familiar with. He *could*, for example reveal himself directly into our minds. He very well *could*, but it must be plain the minute one considers this option, that if he did this very often, it would be impossible to distinguish His thoughts from our own. We may suppose that when people have reported having visions or "receiving the word of the Lord" or what not, they had a way to distinguish what they were experiencing from their normal experience of reality. If God was constantly present via visions, one would not be able to distinguish the visions from the rest of reality. To put it another way, on this view, one could just as easily conclude that these visions were part and parcel of being human. Fish do not know they are wet.

---

[9] Far from a Pauline invention, this concept is expressed elsewhere, including in the Old Testament, such as in Psalm 139.

In the second place, people will point out that historically, miracles have often been associated with revelatory claims, so, why doesn't God perform miracles regularly?

But this also founders on the problem of distinguishing between what is 'normal' and what is 'super-normal.' If miracles happened all the time, one could not actually know when a miracle was happening. If God performed miracles regularly, they would be indistinguishable from what happens regularly. It is only because people cannot walk on water that it is noteworthy when a person does. It is only because one loaf of bread cannot be changed into bread enough to feed five thousand, in the blink of an eye, that the incident catches our attention at all. If dead men got up and walked around all the time, it would not be significant if a particular dead man pointed to his own resurrection as evidence for his divinity.

It is often asserted that people's acceptance of miracles reflects their own gullibility, or, in reference to those in the distant past that have claimed to have seen miracles, a lack of sophistication or ignorance about the laws of nature. However, in the three cases just mentioned, we see that in point of fact, all three of them would be regarded as miracles *today* if they were observed. It is precisely because people in the past understood certain laws of nature that they deemed them miracles in the first place. (They may not have uncovered the mathematics or grasped them all well enough to manipulate them, but they did know them.)

We draw from these two instinctive reactions several important relevant points. First of all, in order for God to reveal himself to us, it must be the case that he does *not* ordinarily reveal himself to us! Second of all, in order that we recognize that it is God communicating with us rather than our fellow man communicating with us, or just the regular operations of nature, there must be a familiar pattern that can be violated so that we can see the deviation. Moreover, the only way we could be sure it was a divine communication was if it was associated with some kind of feat that even humans *could not* reproduce—no matter their scientific knowledge or technical sophistication.

These principles could be expanded on in detail in order to further illustrate that, in the main, the kinds of miracles that turned people's heads that we hear about in the Bible are the kind that would turn our heads, today.

It is worth calling attention to just one more example: fulfilled prophecy. It appears that science fiction and the mathematician's notepad are the only places humans will attain time-travel. It would require time-travel of some sort to accurately predict events in the future that cannot be manipulated into happening by humans, and the wider the gap between the prediction and the event, the less chance that even manipulation can be seriously considered. Thus, associating one's message with a prediction of the future validates the claim that the one talking is a divine messenger or God Himself, but the validation must necessarily come much later. The later the better, actually. But even here, God would have to be crafty.

For example, if in the Old Testament it had been written that the Messiah's name would be "Jesus" you can be certain that every good Jewish boy from the moment of the prophecy until its fulfillment would have been named Jesus. The result being, of course, that when the promised "Jesus" arrives, and is named Jesus, it is trivial and is useless for authenticating the right 'Jesus's' claim to be the Messiah.

Compare and contrast with the prediction in Genesis that the 'scepter would not depart from Judah.' That is, the promised king (for that is what 'messiah' referred to in the Jewish understanding of the term 'king' as 'anointed one') would be born in the family line of Judah, one of the twelve sons of Jacob. Genesis, even on the most liberal of views, was written *long* before the New Testament. The events it records go back beyond 1,000 BC. Later texts explain with some precision where the twelve tribes would settle, allowing more precision in tracking the movements of successive foreign armies, namely the Assyrians and the

Babylonians. The Assyrians would utterly demolish ten of the twelve tribes, scattering them to the four winds, making it impossible to trace one's family line with any certainty after this. Spared were there tribes of Judah and Benjamin, who, about 150 years later, would be conquered by the Babylonians.

The Babylonians, however, did not scatter the Jews. The lineage of those remaining from the tribes of Judah and Benjamin retained their integrity.

Entirely by luck, out of the two tribes that were left, one of them *happened to be* the same predicted hundreds of years earlier to be the eventual source of Israel's rescuing king. While one can imagine the Jews conniving to ensure that Judah would be the 'last man standing' one can't imagine the brutal Assyrians going along with the plan. There is no conceivable way that this particular prophecy could have been manipulated by the ones who were most concerned about it, because the ones most concerned about it were destroyed by ones who cared least about it.

Naturally, to people who have already determined that there can be no truth to such things (because there is no God), these texts cannot be taken at anywhere near face value, for to do so would—obviously—entail direct and unequivocal evidence for the existence of God. Unfortunately, even *they* cannot do away with the archeological evidence for the existence of the "House of David" and the *Assyrian* record of Sennacherib's victories in Palestine.

Another example of fulfilled prophecy placed outside the reach of sympathetic manipulators is the mirroring of Psalm 22 with the events surrounding the crucifixion of Jesus. Certainly, Jesus wished to alert onlookers to the relationship between the Psalm and what was happening to him, indicated by the fact that, while on the cross, he blurted out the first line of the Psalm: "My God, My God, why have you forsaken me?"

The Psalm records the 'piercing' of a man by men who

then cast lots for his clothing, which, *by chance* happens with Jesus, when the Roman guards cast lots for his clothing. If it had been Jewish soldiers doing the dirty deed, one could imagine them contriving to fulfill the prophecy, because they had an invested interest in seeing if fulfilled (although a crucified Messiah isn't quite what they had in mind!). The Romans, of course, could not have cared less. Psalm 22, again, was written many hundreds of years before Jesus was hung on the cross. The fulfillment is brought about by indifferent enemies, not by sympathetic and invested Jews.

These and many other examples serve to validate Jesus' claim that he was God, present on earth *in person*. Capped off, of course, by rising from the dead—which also had been foretold in the Scriptures.

This slight detour into miracles and prophecies was meant to prime the reader to understand that it is one thing to receive a message putatively from God, and quite another thing to believe it is *actually* God delivering the message. It is one thing to come to terms with the existence of a Prime entity, and quite another to be sure it is communicating with its contingent creations. The whole endeavor needs to be carefully calibrated to make such a thing possible—as God certainly would know.

In this vein, it is worth mentioning too that there is an added epistemological benefit arising specifically from the public nature of the events in question. Direct revelation inside one's own skull has problems, already referenced, but beyond the problem of distinguishing God's thought from your own thought, there is the possibility of hallucination. There is also the problem of self-deception: God says something you don't like, so you twist it around until it is something you do like. Heaped on top of this is the difficulty of evaluating the claims of private interpretations that other people claim to have received via direct revelation. Supposing that such direct revelations are rare, as they must necessarily be if they are to be distinguished from the ordinary course of affairs, how would one test someone's claim to have received such a thing?

While the Bible does have its examples of 'private revelation' the most important messages that come putatively from God occur in front of dozens, hundreds, thousands, and even tens of thousands of people. There is the case of the rescue of the Jews from slavery to the Egyptians, which transpired, of course, in front of hundreds of thousands of Jews, but also in view of hundreds of thousands of Egyptians. God spoke directly to Moses, but appeared in view of them all when delivering the Decalogue. In the case of Jesus, prophets and intermediaries were dispensed with altogether, and he walked the earth in plain view of thousands of people. Some miracles were private, to be sure, but the feeding of the five thousand certainly wasn't. Appearing in resurrected form to five hundred people at the same time certainly wasn't private.

The public nature of these revelatory acts mitigate against private corruption, deception, and self-deception. It certainly adds epistemological weight to the claims made in public *and* validated in public. Remember, for example, that the place of Jesus' death and resurrection was in Jerusalem, the very heart of the Jewish people. Jesus was crucified during the Passover holiday when the city would have been engorged with Jews visiting from throughout the Roman empire, and all these Jews would have still been there when the rumors rippled out that Jesus' grave was empty and that he had even been seen alive. It was at another such holiday, the Feast of Weeks (Pentecost), just a few weeks after the Passover, that Jesus' disciples began boldly proclaiming what must have surely already been widely believed.

The reader is invited to compare and contrast these examples with the 'miracle' claims found in other religions. Of particular note in this context are Islam and Mormonism.

There is plenty here for the reader to pursue on his own to explore this side of the issue. As it relates to this present essay, however, I hope the reader realizes on his own that, even if the Messenger is validated as God, the 'message' must somehow be categorically different than our communications with each other. Yet, it cannot be so different as to be unintelligible.

We have already encountered such a problem when we considered how a human might 'communicate' with a computer. The reader certainly is aware of problems related to translation from one language to another. Here we are talking about the Absolute communicating with his creation. Surely 'something' must be lost in the translation? Is there a philosophy, ideology, or theology that predicts this and also provides a model for making sense of it? I submit, again, that Christianity is just the ticket.

A Framework for Reconciling these Difficulties as Found in *Flatland*

To better explain the problem, and at the same time provide a clue on how to resolve it, consider the world of Flatland.

Flatland is a book by 19th century author and theologian Edwin Abbott. In this book, Abbott recounts what happens in the two dimensional world of Flatland when a three dimensional object attempts to communicate with the two dimensional entities. You should see the problem: in order for the three dimensional object to communicate with the two dimensional one, it will have to appear within the two dimensional world, and, when doing so, appear *as* a two dimensional object. The two dimensional entities are thus presented with what seems to be not just an unverifiable claim, but one that is fundamentally irrational.

The object which wishes to communicate is a sphere, which appears as a circle to the Flatlanders. He then endeavors to show how his existence *as more than a circle* is not at all irrational, though the sphere's claims make no sense to the Flatlanders and they wonder how they could conceivably test the claims. The sphere explains that it necessarily follows, from what a sphere *is*, that while it will appear as a circle as it passes through the plane of Flatland, its 'sphere-ness' *can* be verified, because certain predictions can be made, if what the sphere says about himself is correct. Namely, as the sphere passes through the two-dimensional plane of Flatland, he will first appear to them as a single point, then as circle that increases in size until it reaches its full diameter, at which point it will decrease in size until it is again only a point, and then disappear. This is exactly what can be expected when a 'supernatural' entity enters Flatland, which the Flatlanders cannot, in principle, reproduce.

But the key thing to realize, here, is that the 'laws' of Flatland are not violated, nor are they irrational. They are, instead, super-rational.[10] The Flatlanders cannot escape their plane of existence by definition, but notice that a sphere contains infinite planes within it, again, by definition. It is not that the laws of nature, thought, and logic are different for the sphere versus the circle, but rather that the sphere's laws *incorporate* and *transcend* the laws of nature, thought, and logic of Flatland. In order for the sphere to communicate with the circle, the three dimensional communications themselves have to be translated into two dimensional symbols. Even an omnipotent sphere could not escape this reality.

The analogy to our own predicament should be easy to grasp. If there exists an entity that transcends our own, even granting its omnipotence, it would still have to make its appearances to its creations within the same 'plane' of experience that its creations are confined to.

Flatland well illustrates the transcendental aspect of the problem, but it does not treat the additional implications that follow from immanence.

In Flatland, the sphere is able to pass through the two dimensional space of flatland because the sphere and Flatland both exist as separate entities in a shared medium. The significance of this fact is grasped immediately. If a

---

[10] By 'super' of course we have not been meaning 'super' in the sense we think of Superman having superpowers, but of the Latin *supra*, by contrast with the Latin, *sub*.

circle is to a sphere, a sphere is to a... what? That is the transcendental implication, but what if they were not in a shared medium, so that Flatland was itself a plane of existence within the sphere itself and the sphere was all that there was? On this scenario, it would not even be *logically* possible for the sphere to manifest in Flatland as a series of consecutively larger circles until diminishing again into nothing, for that is only *logically* possible in a shared medium! Even operating on super-logical principles. On this view, the sphere is both transcendent and immanent... *over*, *through*, and *in* Flatland.

It doesn't mean that communication and revelation is not possible. It just means that that the predicament will necessitate certain avenues through which it can happen. I should mention, too, that on this scenario, detection is wholly one-directional. That is, it is not conceivably possible for the Flatlanders to directly perceive the sphere as an independent entity, for this could only have been done from a vantage point distinct from the sphere, i.e., somewhere else in the 'shared medium.' In this case, the 'shared medium' is part and parcel, somehow, of the sphere itself. There is no where outside the sphere it can 'stand' separate from the sphere in order to behold it. Flatland cannot go up, but the sphere can go down.

This helps illustrate the problem that the Prime has when and if it desires to communicate with us and also provides some insight into how this problem might be resolved. However, it remains an analogy, and as is usually the case with an analogy, breaks down. After all, spheres are not usually known for their intelligence, let alone their desire to reveal themselves to circles, squares, and triangles.

A Better Model than the Author of Flatland Could Deliver: That of the Author

The Christian scriptures provide another analogy that is much superior. While this analogy too can be expected to be incomplete, it has the advantage of being corroborated by the historical evidence that its central figure supported his claim to divinity by rising from the dead.[11]

The analogy is invoked throughout the Scriptures (old and new).

From John 1:

> In the beginning was the Word, and the Word was with God, and the Word was God. He was in the beginning with God. All things were made through him, and without him was not any thing made that was made. In him was life, and the life was the light of men. The light shines in the darkness, and the darkness has not overcome it.
>
> ...
>
> And the Word became flesh and dwelt among us, and we have seen his glory, glory as of the only Son from the Father, full of grace and truth. ... No one has ever seen God; the only God, who is at the Father's side, he has made him known.

Hebrews 1:

> Long ago, at many times and in many ways, God spoke to our fathers by the prophets, but in these last days he has spoken to us by his Son, whom he appointed the heir of all things, through whom also he created the world. He is the radiance of the glory of God and the exact imprint of his nature, and he upholds the universe by the word of his power.

Genesis 1:

> In the beginning, God created the heavens and the earth. 2 The earth was without form and void, and darkness was over the face of the deep. And the Spirit

---

[11] You try it!

of God was hovering over the face of the waters.
And God *said* ...

In these examples, we see God portrayed as an author that creates through his words and Word. His 'son', Jesus, is identified with the Word, and we are told that it is through the Word that "all things were made" and moreover the universe is presently sustained even now "by the word of his power."[12]

The mode of creation through which authors work is something well known to humanity. Indeed, probably every human, by exercise of his imagination, has direct experience on the relation between the 'author' and the author's creation. The author creates worlds in his mind long before it is translated into symbols by which other authors re-create those worlds by processing those symbols. These worlds are likewise created and sustained by the authors' 'words of power.'

Instead of thinking about how a sphere might reveal itself to a circle in Flatland, consider instead how Abbott, as the author of *Flatland*, could have revealed himself to both sphere and circle! Various avenues were open, but ultimately directly incarnating himself in his own world would be the most efficient and effective way. This sort of phenomena seems so obvious and self-evident that it is almost surprising that Christianity is the only religion that proposes that God has done just this.

In this model, Abbott both transcends and is immanent within his created world, able to do what his sphere never could. But 'powers' are 'lost in the translation.' In Abbott's 'sub-creation,' his characters had certain capabilities, but they were distant shadows of Abbott's capabilities. Even Abbott's own abilities are limited: having free-will himself, he can create characters, but even *he*, he who is omnipotent relative to his creative world, *cannot impart to his creations*

---

[12] Hebrews 1, above.

genuine free will.

Imago Dei

The question naturally arises: just how is it that humans have this creative ability to make (sub)worlds? Monkeys may use sticks for 'tools' but there is no sign that they build worlds, for their own pleasure, or for others. If we did not have revelation, the question would be unanswerable. But with the revelation, we have a coherent account:

> So God created man in his own image,
> in the image of God he created him;
> male and female he created them.

God is the Author, and being made by God in His image, we are authors. The progression goes like this:

Substance — Image — Shadow.

Or:

God — Abbott — Flatland.

Or:

Creator — Creation — Sub-Creation

And so on.

Reflecting on our own experience of 'images' we can grasp how they are often very useful to identify persons, scenes, and objects, but they nonetheless lack certain capabilities that their corresponding 'substance' possesses. For example, a picture of a coffee cup will effectively convey the concept of a coffee cup to another person, but no picture of a coffee cup will hold coffee as well as a the 'real' coffee cup will. Similarly, we cannot impart free-will to our creations (i.e., the picture of a coffee cup), although we ourselves appear to have it (i.e., the actual ability to hold coffee). The free-will Abbot possessed, and we possess, can only be *an image* of the free-will that God has. He, having greater capabilities than we, *can* impart genuine free-will to his creation.

No doubt, thoughts about an infinite regression come to one's mind: is there a 'real' coffee cup that is *more* real than our coffee cups? Once again, logic *requires* us to come to the conclusion of a Prime entity, else our epistemology crumbles.

It is worth pointing out here, relative to what was discussed in Part Two, that on this view we now have a principled reason for believing that our grasp of reality is very high. With Darwinism, we could not tell if our understanding of reality corresponded with 1% or 99% of reality the way it was, but on this view, humans were created in the image of a perfect, rational Being. Presumably, our grasp of reality has become corrupted, just as humanity and all of creation has become corrupted, but at least here we can say we are working our way *down* from 100% rather than *up* from puss and scum.

There is something else that this model brings to the table, and that is the power of words to create, and of language, and the realization that language itself must be seen as subject to 'trans-realities.'

Many philosophers, linguists, and scientists have determined that there very much appears to be a relationship between our minds, language, *and reality itself.* This has led them to propose and seriously consider ideas that seem ludicrous and absurd, but that is because they were only willing to allow the existence of our own plane of reality and no other, much as the Flatlanders insisted (initially) that there was their own two dimensional reality and no other.

Authors know better, even if it is only because they feel it in their bones. They constantly amaze us with their ability to create whole new worlds—and sometimes, they enter into them just as God, in Jesus, is said to have entered into our own. This sort of relationship between words and creation makes sense if in fact authors are themselves made in the image of the Prime Author. If our reality is not the final step in the regression, the difficulties posed by the philosophers disappear, because we no longer have to locate the basis of reality in our own thought.

Now we can see that even our *thought* and *language* must be in the *image* of *Prime Thought* and *Prime Language*. It is no wonder we get confused and turned around in circles! Even our words and rationality is in some sense an 'image' of something Most Real. Even when communicating with each other, we know that something always gets 'lost in *trans*lation.' And here we have the ultimate in translation.

This 'lost in translation' aspect of communication between the Prime Communicator and ourselves has deep philosophical implications, and even creates some problems we need to wrestle with, but it also points the way to some solutions to issues that people have deemed intractable. For example, it is frequently cited by skeptics that the doctrine of the Trinity is a load of nonsense. Theologians themselves have scratched their heads about it. This doctrine, however, is a 'two dimensional' attempt to understand the nature of a 'three dimensional' entity. It is not that it is an irrational doctrine, but rather it is the case that the doctrine employs 'two dimensional' language and rationality (as it must, just as the sphere must appear as a circle to other circles) to comprehend something that is only comprehensible according to *super-rationality*. In short, we could never, in principle, comprehend it. The best that we can do is approximate it.

But even if not for the fact that the Triune God revealed his Triune nature to his creation, we would still be able to deduce that the real nature of the Prime would always have been 'more' than our words could have captured.

In fact, insofar as many of the world's religions are 'rational' and 'comprehensible,' that is actually a point *against* them. There is nothing particularly difficult to grasp about Zeus or the Pantheon. These can easily be understood within the terms of our 'plane of existence.' Zeus is just like the superhero, Superman. Hinduism and Buddhism are variations of the same. Only Christianity posits the integrity of the 'rational' by appeal to the existence of the 'super-rational,' where, by *necessity*, our doctrines and teachings must forever be 'images' or even 'shadows' of the things they ultimately represent.

I would submit that if this is not so, then there is no hope at all for us knowing *anything*.

WHY DOES A GOOD AND ALL-POWERFUL GOD[13] ALLOW SUFFERING?

I've read that very wealthy or powerful people are sometimes concerned that their friends are more interested in their money or power than who they are as individuals. How might such a person, desiring genuine companionship, seek to resolve this problem? History and fairytale provide some clues, but we probably don't need their help, since some answers present themselves intuitively. For example, in the Prince and the Pauper, the rich and powerful prince passes himself off as a poor person to see the world as it really is, without the world constantly trying to ingratiate itself with the prince.

I would like the reader to stop for a moment and think carefully about this. If you had this 'problem' would it not be the case that you would seek to conceal your wealth and power from those you hope to make into close friends, until those friends have proved their mettle? I leave aside, of course, those who want to use their wealth and power to gain them friends, but surely such a person is aware of the tradeoff—their new friends may like them *only* because of the wealth and power—and is prepared to accept the reality of that program.

There is a line of argument common among atheists that, if there is a God, believers should have measurably better lives than unbelievers. Believers should not get sick as often as unbelievers. Believers should be more fortunate in their professional life than unbelievers. When the believer prays, the fruits of that prayer should be obvious, or at least, discernable. Believers should live longer. Believers should not suffer—after all, their best friend is an all-loving, all-powerful, all-knowing God.

There have, interestingly enough, been studies that seem

---

[13] Pardon the redundancy.

to suggest benefits of generic 'belief' but the implications, should these studies be accurate, are not very extensive or impressive. A hospital, for example, may see the wisdom of making sure that people's spiritual needs are being met while a patient is in their care, but can you see a hospital making proselytizing part of its policy? Or, can you see an atheist concluding from such studies that the health benefit of belief warrants their conversion?

Having read an awful lot of atheist rebuttals of what are usually caricatures of "Pascal's Wager," I think it is safe to say that there is not a widespread movement among non-believers to become believers just because they might heal faster or what not. But what if they did? Would anyone, including the atheist himself, conceive of his 'belief' as commendable?

If in fact it was the case that it was discernable that believers did not get sick as often as unbelievers, that believers were more wealthy and powerful than unbelievers, that the believers had more satisfying professional lives, more domestic tranquility, lived longer, and, chiefly, did not suffer, and with this evidence in hand the atheist became a 'believer,' would anyone view this conversion as anything other than an act of pure self-interest?

How would this not be the same as becoming someone's friend only because that person was rich and powerful?

It is probably not a coincidence that the argument is often put in these terms, that is, 'believer' versus 'unbeliever,' rather than 'Christian' versus 'non-Christian.' The well-being of all religionists is set against non-religionists for the purpose of the study. The actual veracity of the belief system is not important, rather, the effects of the religious state of mind, or the actual structure of the brain, are the chief subject matter. In other words, for the purposes of such studies, whether or not there actually *is* a 'rich and powerful' entity that really exists and is a proper object of 'friendship' matters far less than the fact that the person *believes* that entity really exists.

If, however, there *is* a 'rich and powerful entity' on the other side of this equation, one can see how that could significantly alter the whole dynamic. Moreover, the moment you narrow things down specifically to a particular 'entity,' you are necessarily bound to consider the individual personality of that entity, and cannot spin hypothetical scenarios endlessly. This is the same as if one were first talking about the preferences of people in general and switch to talking about, say, George Smith of 103 Union Street. Sure, the 'rich and powerful' entity may be of the sort that does not care at all if people pledge their allegiance to it for purely mercenary reasons. It may, however, be the sort that desires genuine friendships. How might we ever know which is the case?

Now, the moment one goes beyond the wide field of 'generic belief' to the very specific and narrow case of Christianity, one is compelled to examine the precise claims of Christianity in considering these issues. If there is anything absolutely clear from the Christian scriptures, it is that there is no promise *at all* that the Christian will be spared pain and suffering, or will experience 'better' lives than others, or that prayers will always have the effect one desires.

If anything, it is exactly the opposite. Suffering is part and parcel of the Christian walk. For example, Jesus said: "If anyone would come after me, let him deny himself and take up his cross and follow me." (Matthew 16:24). Carrying a cross is not easy work, and usually ended in a crucifixion. The apostle Paul put suffering in perspective in Romans 8, where he quoted from Psalm 44: "For your sake we are being killed all the day long; we are regarded as sheep to be slaughtered." The unknown author of Hebrews wrote in chapter 11 of 'heroes' of the faith:

> Some were tortured, refusing to accept release, so
> that they might rise again to a better life. Others

suffered mocking and flogging, and even chains and imprisonment. They were stoned, they were sawn in two, they were killed with the sword. They went about in skins of sheep and goats, destitute, afflicted, mistreated— of whom the world was not worthy— wandering about in deserts and mountains, and in dens and caves of the earth.

Do the lives of the faithful described in Hebrews 11, seem 'better' to you? It is hard to read the Bible earnestly and honestly and come away with the belief that it predicts clear sailing to believers. One is left scratching his head as to how someone might possibly think such a thing. And as far as the efficacy of the believer's prayers, though it is promised that God hears the Christian's prayers, the Bible also explicitly states that *only the ones consistent* with God's will are going to be acted on (see 1 John 5:14). The reader may recall that Jesus prayed in the garden of Gethsemane that he be spared the cup of suffering—if it be his Father's will. By the grace of God, it wasn't.

From these passages and many others that can be produced, it can thus be shown that the whole line of argument offered by the skeptic, as it relates to Christianity, at least, is sheer nonsense. There is very little in Christianity to suggest that what the atheists think one ought to expect if Christianity is true is what Christianity really predicts. What there is we shall address presently, but there is another important consideration.

We have been thinking about this issue from the perspective of the really existing 'rich and powerful' entity trying to gather around it individuals who wish to be its 'friend' out of sincere affection, and not merely because they want to get something out of the relationship. An obvious approach for the 'rich and powerful entity' is to conceal the wealth and power from others. But what if the wealth and power cannot be concealed? And what if there is no desire on the part of the other individuals to be 'friends' with the 'rich and powerful entity' in the first place?

We can easily conceive of such a situation in regards to an American president. It doesn't matter which you choose, for it is unlikely that any American president would be unrecognized for who he is and just as likely that there will be large swaths of the population who have no interest whatsoever in taking that person as a friend. More than that, many of these people hold that president in outright contempt.

God is very much in this situation, with some very important differences. First of all, if there is a God and he is as Christians describe him, there is no way to escape his presence. God transcends the created order but also is fully immanent within it, as well. Ephesians 4 says:

> There is [...] one God and Father of all, who is *over* all and *through* all and *in* all.

If you understand God's non-contingent nature then you understand that it *must* be this way. The moment you grasp what, *who*, it is we are talking about, there is no real way to ignore the great power and majesty of the one in question. The president may have great power and wealth, but he still puts on his pants one leg at a time just like the rest of us. He is still very small when compared to nearly anything else in the created order, such as the sun, a supernova, or a hurricane. God is the very creator of the created order!

On the Christian's understanding of the matter, God is non-contingent and the only real thing that is non-contingent. That means that every corner of the universe, no matter how distant, small, or large, being contingent, is at this very moment, and every moment, sustained by the full knowledge and might of God.[14] However, while you cannot escape his presence, it is possible to shut out your awareness of his

---

[14] See Hebrews 1:3.

presence. On this understanding of who God is, we see that this possibility is not a necessity—it could have been otherwise. Let us consider carefully what this would be like.

If it were the case that each of us were constantly and perpetually aware of the immediate presence of God Almighty, then there would not be any room for anything less than our full allegiance to Him in every respect. One would have no basis whatsoever for challenging him on policy matters—consider again the case of the American president that you despise, but now imagine that he is also the maker of the entire universe, and hence is definitely and definitively correct on every matter, large and small. Any disagreement that you have could not possibly be based on reality. It would have to have some other source: sheer obstinacy. To put it bluntly, to have your politics diverge from an omnipotent and omniscient president is to engage in open rebellion, a blatant refusal to accept reality as it really is and insist on a reality that could never, by definition, be.

But what could we say about the quality of your loyalty if faced with the 100% knowledge that there is no basis for being loyal to anyone or anything else? If you obey *this* president's dictates when he is watching your every move, including every movement of your mind, and you can actually be aware of his being aware of your actions and your thoughts, can your obedience really be credited as obedience or your loyalty credited as loyalty?

To see the matter clearly we may benefit by changing our metaphor.

Imagine a parent telling a child that he is not to eat a cookie that is on the kitchen table. There is no question in the child's mind that the parent is able to enforce this command, as the parent has in times past directly intervened to prevent certain acts of disobedience. There is no question that the parent has the ability to levy a consequence for disobedience, as that has likely happened as well. If the child takes the cookie *while the parent is in the room*, this act can only be seen as one of willful defiance. If the child does not take the cookie while the parent is in the room, can the child be credited for his obedience? Do we have any reason to think the child does not do so out of genuine love and respect for the parent?

No.

The only conceivable way that this 'higher motive' can be cultivated and demonstrated is for the parent to remove himself from the room.

Now, the reader might protest, saying that we are talking about an omnipotent and omniscient 'parent.' While we mere mortals would not have any way to know what basis the child's obedience rests, God-as-Parent certainly would know, and would not need to 'leave the room' in order to obtain this knowledge. Let us concede it, but remember that God, like the parent, is not only concerned about his own knowledge. In short, could the *child* know his obedience is true obedience if the parent is sitting there watching his every move? God-as-Parent may know the genuine motives of the child without removing himself from the scene, but in order for the *child* to know, it is still required that the Parent leave the kitchen.

Now, once the Parent does leave the kitchen, leaving the child alone with the cookie, a whole new universe of possibilities open up for the child. The child can engage in that time-tested analysis, "Did the Parent *really say*..." or could attempt to rationalize the taking of the cookie based on some bit of specious reasoning such as "I am so hungry, I could die... if I do not take the cookie, I will die... my Parent wouldn't want me to die, would he?" If, seemingly alone in this new universe, the child does not take the cookie, the *child* knows his obedience was real, and not an illusion.

The reader may further protest that 'fear of consequence' is a far cry from 'love and respect.' There is no reason to deny that. Even so, as most parents can attest to, 'fear of consequence' is the necessary preliminary stage before 'love and respect' is reached. Even if parents thought it were theoretically possible to skip this stage, most have discovered that in actual practice, it cannot be skipped. Still, there comes a point where the child is grown enough where the parents have very little leverage over the child except 'love and respect.'

There is in some quarters debate over the morality and wisdom of a parent spanking their young child, but there has never been, to my knowledge, a similar concern about a father taking his forty-year old son over his knee to administer some sound corporal punishment. What began as 'fear of consequence' could not remain so forever, but 'fear of consequence' proved to be the necessary and important training for what would eventually become what could only remain as a basis for loyalty and allegiance, 'love and respect.'

It is probably no accident that we read in the book of Proverbs, "The fear of the Lord is the beginning of wisdom." After all, obeying your parent's commands when you yourself have only been alive for a few years is a good strategy for remaining alive. Eventually, fear gives way to 'love and respect' and wisdom, as the toddler matures, marries, and imparts to his own children what was first given to him.

We have been exploring the nature of the loyalty, love, and obedience as to whether or not these can be considered real and genuine if in fact they are coerced, and also whether or not the two parties can themselves know if they are real and genuine. We have only touched on something else that is of equal significance: willful defiance.

The parent knows exactly what I mean, but most readers will be able to grasp it with just a few short examples.

> Situation A. The parent has left a plate of cookies on the table and has given no instructions or commands regarding them to the child. A few moments later, the child enters the kitchen, sees the cookie, and takes and eats.

Situation B. The parent has left a plate of cookies on the table and has expressly forbidden the child from eating one of the cookies. A few moments later, the parent leaves the room. The child snatches one of the cookies and eats it.

Situation C. The parent has left a plate of cookies on the table and has expressly forbidden the child from eating one of the cookies. The parent sits down at the table and gives full attention to the plate of the cookies. In the parent's presence, the child takes the cookie and eats it.

I believe that most readers will intuitively understand that the consequences the child warrants in each of these situations are diverse, both in their nature and in their degree. In Situation A., the child has not received instruction so can hardly be faulted for doing something that, presumably, the parent did not want. In Situation B, the child has defied the parent, but not in the parent's presence. Parents know they can expect any manner of rationalizations from the child once the transgression has been discovered, but regardless, the fact that the child waited until the parent left the room indicates at least some kind of respect for the parent. In Situation C, there isn't the slightest space for fear, love, or respect to factor into the situation—from the child's perspective.

If Situation B at least provided the necessary test to see if the love, loyalty, and devotion were real and genuine, in Situation C, no test is necessary. The child has shown his cards plainly, and defies the parent to do something about it. We have passed out of the realm of wondering about the nature of the relationship between the parent and child into a consideration of the character and moral fiber of the child alone. Setting aside any questions about why the child felt it could behave in this way, it remains the case that the behavior reveals the child to be wholly obstinate, rebellious, and hard-hearted. If in Situations A and B there were room for empathy or mercy, this has been stripped away in Situation C. Indeed, the transgression in Situation A is of an entirely different category than the transgression in Situation C. In Situation A, it was only a matter of taking a cookie without express permission, but from there, in increasing degrees from B to C, there is the additional, much more serious matter, of taking the cookie *and* the outright defiance in the face of a clear command.

I would wager that most parents would have a different response for each of these three situations. How they would proceed to discipline the child in Situation A would be different than what they would do in Situation B, and would be yet more distinct in Situation C. How, now, if the parent actually *expects* the child, for one reason or another, to act in willful defiance? That is, if the parent *expects* the child to take the cookie, even with the parent present, how shall the parent proceed?

If the parent does remain in the room to witness the transgression, the parent's hand is forced; the die is cast, and mercy is hardly the first or best option. So long as the parent arranges so that only Situation B occurs, even if repeatedly and often, the harshest measures that would be warranted by Situation C can be avoided. If the parent has reason to believe, for one reason or another, that the child is in a state to be completely irascible and belligerent, and the parent loves and cares for the child and doesn't particularly care for administering harsh discipline when it can be avoided, the parent may try to keep things from escalating into the point of no return for as long as possible.

And yet, eventually, the parent has got to go back into the kitchen. It is the *parent's* kitchen, after all. There are some who insist that there is no reason why God should not just wait forever to keep this climactic confrontation from occurring. Returning to our analogy, the presumption is that the 'disobedient child' has some legitimate claim to be left alone within the 'house.' But this is absurd. The adults own the house and the child has no legitimate right to expect or demand some part of it as their exclusive domain. The universe is God's. He made it. He sustains it. It is only out of compassion that He does not assert His rights to it at all points and in all areas, but it is as unreasonable to think he ought to refrain forever from doing so, just as it is unreasonable to think a parent should eternally cede some space in their own house to some other person.

The above analysis is predicated on the parent having good reason to be concerned about the child's behavior. Presumably, a child that didn't have a disobedient bone in him who also possessed complete knowledge about what is good and bad for him is one where Situation A would be all that is necessary. That is, before sin was in the world, there would be little need for the preceding discussion, for there would have been little need for the Parent to moderate His presence and absence... though, *a little*. But sin *is* in the world. The Family harmony has been thrown completely out of sorts. The Parent will have to take the above considerations into account—for each and every person.

Skeptics can often be heard declaring that they would have no problems throwing their lot in with God if only God would make his presence irrefutably obvious and plain. They reason that since that is God's desire, He would simply do the one thing needful. What they do not take account is whether or not they are really ready for that direct manifestation. Indeed, some atheists have even declared that even if God made himself undeniably apparent, they would still steadfastly oppose God. Their disobedience, then, would be in the category that we called Situation C. If God demanded loyalty supremely, then He could certainly acquire it. If He also desires love, then He will postpone the confrontation for as long as it can be postponed.

When one is on the lookout for such considerations, one discovers these dynamics are frequently in play within the Christian Scriptures. There are several instances in particular which are informative.

There is, in the first place, the case of Pharaoh. The

complaint has sometimes been made that Pharaoh did not receive a fair treatment, as the Scriptures report that "God hardened Pharaoh's heart." A closer reading of the text, however, reveals that before God hardened Pharaoh's heart, Pharaoh had already hardened his own heart several times. Each plague sent upon the Egyptians seems to target one of the pantheon of Egyptian gods who appear incapable of preventing the God of Moses from doing His worst. Pharaoh sought and received evidence that the God of Moses was in fact the God of the universe and still remained in rebellion. We may entertain theories as to why Pharaoh continued to be obstinate. My theory is that Pharaoh believed the hype that Pharaoh was himself the greatest of all the gods. Thus, if each plague was tailored to trump one of the Egyptian gods, the final demonstration would have to trump Pharaoh himself as god. Pharaoh proved unable to prevent the life of his own firstborn from being taken or—and the Egyptians certainly noticed this—the lives of the firstborn in all of Egypt from being taken. By this time, however, Pharaoh had already proved that he would remain in open rebellion regardless of the evidence submitted. When God did finally harden Pharaoh's heart, he did it in a particular direction, so as to glorify Himself as He rescued the Jews.

The account reveals that there was a cost to this direct appearance by the God of Moses.

It was not only the case that the Egyptians were left without excuse. The Jews themselves were left without excuse. Thus, the consequences of their own later rebellion while under the direction of Moses was akin to our Situation B. There could be no doubt that the God of Moses was real and as described, as the God of Moses had revealed himself to them all in a powerful demonstration. The consequences of their rebellion were, understandably, severe.

Later readers would like to think that these rebellious Jews were stupid and those of us alive today would not make the same blunders, but the moral of the story is to understand that it is entirely possible *today* for God to reveal himself directly and still have people remain defiant. God may prefer not obliterating us, therefore it is wise if He refrains from such direct manifestations.

There is, in the second place, the case of Saul, who would become known as Paul. It does not appear that Saul was a direct witness to the events concerning Jesus life and resurrection, although he was a contemporary. When Christianity was spreading like wildfire, it was chiefly among his fellow Jews. As a devout Jew, and mindful of the holiness that the God of Moses demanded, he did what he thought was best, namely hunting down the wayward Jews and murdering them. Then, on the road to Damascus, Jesus revealed himself directly to Saul.

From the foregoing, it will be instantly recognized that in doing so, Jesus took a risk. Faced with the overwhelming evidence that Christianity wasn't a Jewish heresy but rather truth itself, Saul could have refused to throw his lot in with God-as-He-really-was and instead clung to the comfortable beliefs about God-as-Saul-imagined-Him-to-be.

Presumably, there was something about Saul that Jesus thought the risk worth taking, and in this case, at least, we did not see open rebellion as the reaction, but rather, love and fealty. Given Paul's profound impact on the trajectory of Christianity, we may suppose that in his case the gamble paid off.

A sobering implication is that if Jesus likewise gambled with the rest of us, even if we gave God our devotion, our contribution to the cause would be, by comparison, minimal. Or, perhaps it is the case that, as is being submitted in this essay, more people would be lost forever by such a display than would ultimately be saved.

Finally, there is the case of Jesus himself. Jesus claimed to be God incarnate, but not immediately. He sort of dribbled out the implications over the course of His ministry, and likewise, His demonstrations. He left room for doubt, and from the above analysis, the reader can understand why. As things reached their climax, however, less and less room could be allowed.

There was the case of Jesus hurtling the demons out of the man with the Jewish elites declaring that the demons were thrown out by the power of Beelzebub, rather than accepting Jesus' own explanation. In this instance, Jesus warns that there is only one unforgiveable sin, the Blasphemy against the Holy Spirit. We learn that this blasphemy is not the mere invocation of words, but rather open rebellion in the face of irrefutable evidence, crediting some other entity rather than the entity everyone knows is really present and responsible: God Himself. Blasphemy of the Holy Spirit is when someone hardens their own heart, thus putting themselves, by their own reason and strength, outside the reach of God's love and mercy.

When Jesus performed one of his greatest feats, the raising of Lazarus from the dead, the point of decision had essentially been reached. The die was cast. The Jewish elites refused to change their minds and instead at that moment realized that Jesus must die. After this final hardening of their hearts, we may read between the lines and see that from that moment on, God hardened their hearts in particular directions so as to glorify Himself in a particular manner.

Shortly before going to His death, Jesus told His disciples that He would die and rise, but then, He would *leave*, and this would actually be better for them, for He would instead send the Holy Spirit. This must have been inexplicable to the disciples. Surely, victorious in the end it would make much more sense to establish a throne in Jerusalem and remain in view of humanity from then on? If loyalty and allegiance were all that was desired, perhaps so. But what if that was not all that was desired? From the above we can see that Jesus' leaving was not just better for the disciples, but was better for all of us. If Jesus remained on His throne today where all could see him at every moment, it would be impossible to determine whether or not we were His friends out of sincere affection, or for mercenary reasons. God, surely, would know, but *we* wouldn't.

We have now returned full circle to the analogy that we began the essay with, but with some important distinctions in hand. The entity in question, God, is no mere 'rich and powerful' person. Assuming that this entity actually exists, He is the maker and creator of the entire universe and has legitimate claim to every atom within it. It is absurd to think that there is some space we can reserve as our own, whether that 'space' be physical, emotional, mental, or spiritual. Yet, except for occasional claims of divine intrusions into our collective history, backed with varying degrees of substantiation, there have been not been overwhelming and persistent, and therefore irrefutable, manifestations of His presence.

I would submit that this is *exactly* what one would expect if the Christian understanding of God is *actually* the case.

To be absolutely clear what the 'this' refers to, it is: Mankind has fallen into rebellion against a transcendent, immanent, omnipotent, omniscient, and omni-benevolent being that wishes to restore each person into a healthy relationship with Him, and knows that direct appearances in each and every case would definitively destroy the chances of such a restoration in many of those cases. He has not been wholly absent, but his appearances have been calculated such that they ultimately built up to a point where He appeared personally, as a human, to make his case in terms we can relate to without being flash-hardened, performed an ultimate demonstration, and then... left. With that ultimate demonstration now firmly embedded in the annals of human history, with sufficient evidence to accept that those events are real facts of history, it remains sufficiently ambiguous to allow some room for doubt—for now.

While on the Christian view it would seem that God has fully committed the establishment of his kingdom to the testimony of those first witnesses and the continuing work of those who accept that testimony, one can still entertain the line of argument that supposes that some small-scale divine intrusions ought to occur, at least occasionally.

A wide survey of human experience past and present seems to suggest that this is in fact happening, but, as is usually the case, it satisfies no one. That is to say, the skeptics among us like to insist that in today's 'scientific' age, superstitions and mysticism ought to be a thing of the past, yet they themselves will be among the first to collect, and—always—attempt to debunk, such accounts. In other words, millions of people alive today attest to having had 'incidents' that defy a strictly naturalistic view of existence, but the response to this is not to allow this as evidence against a strictly naturalistic view, but as evidence for the stupidity and gullibility of their fellow man.

What is strange indeed, however, is when these hard-minded atheistic skeptics themselves have these experiences, and do not give them their due weight. After all, since we are talking about 'hard-minded atheistic skeptics' we are, by definition, ruling out the stupid and gullible, right?

In my years of having conversations with atheists, or listening in on other conversations, I have had on more than one occasion heard them talking about strange encounters they may have had. I have even seen on the Internet the occasional atheist that is firmly convinced in the existence of ghosts. Only in the last decade, however, have I had atheists that I could count as friends relate to me that they have had such experiences. That is, while what I'm about to relate may be characterized as 'hear-say' to the reader, it is second-hand to me. But before I relate these second-hand stories, I wish to relate a first-hand story from one of my own experiences.

When I went to college it was with the goal of becoming a pastor. However, very early on, I struggled with intense doubts about the very existence of God. There was, in fact, a period in which I would have described myself as an atheist. But even after returning to the faith, I was reluctant to devote my life to full-time ministry without having absolute knowledge that God was real and was as I understood Him through the Scriptures. There were two cases where God provided me with the demonstration that I needed, one of which I will now share.

It was one evening after a prayer vigil that I was leading that doubts came upon me hard and fast. Hearing the deep pains expressed in the prayer requests, I told God that I could not in good faith attest to His sufficiency in addressing those requests based on my conviction that the Christian Scriptures really recounted real history. I insisted on a demonstration, and I had the audacity to even set the terms of the demonstration.

"God," I said, "I will take this lit candle out to my dormitory, and if it remains lit the entire time, then I will proceed with full assurance of your existence."

This might seem like a weak test, but the reader must understand that to get to my dormitory, I would need to walk some 500 yards, most of it on a road not far from the bluffs of Lake Michigan. It is usually quite windy on that road, and it was quite windy on that night.

So, I took that lit candle for a walk, studiously refraining from using my other hand to block the wind. More than once it seemed as though it were going to be snuffed out. I made it all the way to the front door of the dormitory, and had just gotten to a place where the wind was actually blocked by the doorway entrance—when it went out!

I laughed out loud, for even in that moment I understood that God had met the terms of my demonstration, but not completely. Right at the end, He left me with room for doubt. The candle had stayed lit when it shouldn't have stayed lit and went out when it should have stayed lit: the decision was mine to make at that moment... harden my heart, or surrender it. That evening, I surrendered it.

I don't even bother asking for such demonstrations any more. Besides revealing my own faithlessness, it would be rude.

I told you that story to set the table, as it were, for the stories of my two atheist friends who have had their own 'encounters.'

In the first example, the friend sent me a message asking for my phone number, saying he needed to talk to me urgently. A short time later, he called me and related to me some incidents that had unnerved him greatly.

It turns out that a friend of his, whom he had converted from Christianity to atheism, had died in a motorcycle wreck. He and his friend had made a 'deal' that whomever died first would try to get a message to the other if they had been wrong about the whole 'theism' thing. Not long afterwards, he was in the garage and heard his friend call out his name—loudly—right behind him. He turned, and, as the reader will predict, saw no one. This, incidentally, turns out to be a fairly common human experience. As the reader will further predict, since it is common, instead of allowing these experiences to weigh against a strictly naturalistic understanding of the world, skeptics have instead dismissed them as hallucinations, and such.

My friend, as skeptical as the rest, was quite prepared to dismiss his experience as just this kind of common hallucination, except that there was another experience on top of that one. According to him, he received a phone call from his dead friend's cell phone. Playing on the line was one of their favorite songs. My friend knew it was his friend's cell phone because he had caller-ID. Moreover, it had been his job, after his friend died, to disconnect his friend's cell phone service!

When my friend called me up and related this to me, I asked him what he expected me to contribute, as it seemed that he had all that he needed already. He had asked for a sign and had received it. All that was left was to surrender. His reply: "Sure, maybe this shows that there is a God or god of some sort, but *which* God?" I put myself at his service in trying to answer that question but warned him about dismissing his experience, the experience of the Pharaoh firmly in mind.

Several years later we re-connected. He could not dismiss the whole thing as a hallucination but insisted instead that it had to have been a hoax. He didn't know how it was done, or who did it, but *it had to be a hoax*. Given the implications, and his state of mind at the time, one would have thought he would have sought to investigate those questions immediately, but instead he set the matter aside. Today, it is impossible for him to ever rule out the possibility of a hoax, because none of the records and other means that might have been available to him remain open to him to carry out such an investigation.

He asked, God delivered—but left room for doubt. If my friend had really thought it was a hoax, I personally don't think God would have been bothered at all if he had tried to expose it as such. But no investigation was made. Instead, my friend hardened his heart. Not surprisingly, he has experienced other 'strange' encounters since then, but remains unconvinced. He wonders why God doesn't just display Himself in all His glory, but my prayer is that God doesn't; I suspect very much that if this happened, the die would be cast, and my friend lost forever.

The second incident involves an atheist friend who woke up from a deep sleep one night, weeping with grief, as though he had just lost a loved one. A couple of days later, he learned that a friend had committed suicide some days earlier. Some days after *that*, he remembered that he had woken up and wept—it could have been precisely at the moment when his friend committed suicide. Unfortunately, he cannot now recall precisely the night when he had woken up and wept!

Unfortunately?

If the timing had been that perfect, so perfect as to be beyond coincidence, my friend would have had a point of decision put in front of him where to choose the purely naturalistic account would have been to willfully and deliberately deny his own experience of reality. This, ironically, is a friend who has put in his tagline on a discussion forum we frequent a quote—from me!—warning people about denying their own experience of reality! But the timing was not perfect... or at least, if it was perfect, it is now impossible to know for certain that it was perfect... and there remains some room for doubt.

For *now*.

These two atheist friends of mine have received a gift, but within the gift, another gift. They each received direct experiences that were not consistent with a strictly naturalistic account of reality. That was a gift. Within those experiences, there remained some ambiguity. That was the gift whereby God allowed them the dignity of having a free choice.

As it stands, however, both friends have chosen to act on the second gift by dismissing the first gift.

Is it no wonder, given such states of affairs, that God would choose not to dispense overwhelming manifestations upon all who doubt? He must woo, or else He may destroy. It is a tender business, this making friends out of rebels, and lovers out of adulterers.

God does not overwhelmingly reveal Himself *now*, but as already mentioned, there is no reason to think He will forever, or that he ought to. There is also no reason to think that He does not reveal Himself to some extent, *now*, but good reason to think that when and if He does, there will always be some ambiguity to it and some room for doubt. It has been hinted that the chief and primary way that He chooses to reveal Himself *these days* is not through these 'divine intrusions' at all, but rather through the testimony of those who witnessed the first great 'intrusion' when He delivered the Jews out of Egypt and the last great 'intrusion,' God's direct appearance on earth. In these two intrusions we observe a pattern, whereby God begins with small demonstrations and builds up to larger and greater demonstrations until a point of no return comes, when to refuse allegiance and fealty becomes silly and absurd and irrevocably wicked.

These two great 'intrusions' proceeded upon a shared framework of progressive revelation. May I submit that in the lead up to the third great 'intrusion' the same framework will be employed. The skeptics like to say that one of the supreme virtues of the scientific method is that it makes predictions that can be tested. That is precisely what I am doing here—making a prediction that can be tested.

There is a passage in Paul's letter to the Romans that says,

> For what can be known about God is plain to them, because God has shown it to them. For his invisible attributes, namely, his eternal power and divine nature, have been clearly perceived, ever since the creation of the world, in the things that have been made. So they are without excuse.

According to Paul, one can set aside completely the question of 'special revelation,' that is, God directly manifesting without intermediaries. Nature *itself* testifies to the existence of God and at least some of His characteristics. It is common to hear that 'science' has made belief in God superfluous at best and ridiculously absurd, at worst, but in point of fact the discoveries made by mankind over the centuries have made nature's testimony to God's existence and some of his characteristics increasingly and progressively *more* certain and *more* convincing. This is consistent with the pattern described above.

But if this is the case, why are there others who believe exactly the opposite? The answer to this has already been given, and it has less to do with the strength of the evidence, and more to do with the obstinacy of those who perceive it. If the pattern holds, we may expect the strength of the evidence to increase to a point where it becomes simply undeniable. The ones who deny it at that point will reveal to everyone, including themselves, that their disbelief is a matter of choice, and not a matter of the evidence.

To see that this pattern has been unfolding for some time,

we may begin by looking a little at the miracles that Jesus did prior to his death and resurrection. A hardened cynic has once said that any sufficiently technologically advanced race would appear to the less advanced as 'gods.' Any genuine 'miracles' will eventually be reproduced at will by scientists utilizing the latest technology. This mentality was clearly at work in the case where I gave sufficient evidence to an atheist that the resurrection of Jesus was a historical fact. He finally conceded the historicity of the event, but retorted that it remained nonetheless more reasonable to assume that Jesus had been abducted by aliens or perhaps was a space alien. (Really.)

The clear insinuation of this line of argument is that people in the past were total dupes who had little to no understanding about the laws of nature. This view of past humans is encapsulated in the dismissive characterization of the authors of the Christian scriptures as 'ancient goat herders.' Yet, a review of the miracles performed by Jesus shows us that many of them would be considered miraculous today. That is to say, what Jesus is said to have done is impossible even according to the known laws of physics. More importantly, from what we know about the laws of physics today, those feats could *never* be done, by any person or 'sufficiently advanced race.'

Take, for example, Jesus walking on water. If witnessed today, witnesses would be just as amazed today as the 'ancient goat herders' were two thousand years ago. A better example, perhaps, is the feeding of the five thousand. This is a clear violation of the Law of Conservation of mass and energy, and at this point, no one expects this Law to be overthrown—except in science fiction, the only place where such violations can ever be expected to take place. There was a time when it could be objected that Jesus made use of special technology to create matter out of nothing, but that time has long passed. We have learned that such creation *ex nihilo* is just not possible—except, of course, to God.

Similarly, it has sometimes been said that in ancient

times, people could not comprehend when people were really dead. Ironically, such questions bedevil us today. What we do know, however, is that once death really happens, a chain of events occurs in the body immediately and irreversibly with such cataclysmic consequences that resuscitation is just not possible. I am reminded of the skeptic that insisted Jesus could not have risen from the dead, citing just these considerations. He seemed to be unaware that it was precisely this kind of physical impossibility that made the resurrection a worthy corroboration of Jesus' claim to divinity. Moreover, it turns out that the 'ancient goat herders' were right then and would be right today: dead men do not rise.

So, if a man *did* rise from the dead, it could only signify that the power of one not bound to the laws of nature, such as ourselves, or, presumably, space aliens, was at work. Namely, God *had* to be involved.

It seems to have escaped attention among the skeptical community that in order to even recognize a 'divine intrusion' *at all*, it is *necessary* that such 'intrusions' be *rare* and that such 'intrusions' be generally of the sort that are in complete defiance of what is possible according to the orderly patterns of nature, what we have termed "the laws of physics." The most compelling demonstrations will be of the sort that even a race that had 100% knowledge of the laws of physics and 100% capability to manipulate those laws would be unable to duplicate.

A violation of the Law of Conservation would be one such example. Escaping the one-way arrow of time, which we may roughly equate with the law of entropy, and predicting events long in the future, would be another example. Time travel is another one of those things that no one seriously expects to happen except in a work of science fiction; the universe as it is actually observed precludes even the possibility of being able to see the future with precision, let alone travel to it. Thus, someone making a prediction about a future event, otherwise known as 'prophesying,' is claiming to do something that according to the laws of nature simply *cannot* be done. Even 'ancient goat herders' knew this, which is why when they watched predictions come true that had been made decades and even centuries earlier—long after the people who made the predictions died in many cases—they paid attention. We would pay attention today.

Setting aside the great amount of fulfilled prophecy that led the first century Jews to believe that Jesus was just who he said he was, there was also Jesus' own prediction about the destruction of Jerusalem, which would occur some forty years later. This is recorded in the Gospel of Matthew, an account that goes to great pains to show how Jesus fulfilled prophecy and explicitly states in numerous occasions, "this happened in order that the word of such and such prophet would be fulfilled." But when we get to Jesus' prediction about the destruction of Jerusalem, the author fails to give any hint that the predicted event had already taken place, vindicating Jesus yet again.

This wars against the attempts of modern Jesus 'scholars' to make the date of composition much later because obviously the author of Matthew would have wanted to draw attention to Jesus' most notable fulfilled prophecy, but did not. This strongly suggests that that Matthew was written before the fall of Jerusalem (c. 70 AD) just as the evidence has suggested for nearly two thousand years.

The writers of the works included in the New Testament made somewhat frequent assertions about future events. Theoretically, this could allow us to test their veracity and the divinity of their sources, but of course we may not all be alive when these events transpire. We would be wise, nonetheless, to keep watch.

Perhaps the most significant modern developments that point significantly—some would say, overwhelmingly—towards the existence of God, concerns our knowledge of the genome and biochemistry. Skeptics like to say that Darwinism has shown that there is no reason to infer from biology the existence of a Designer, but the majority of their fellow humans have to cover their mouths to keep from laughing when they hear such things.

One such skeptic has insisted that Darwin finally made it possible to be an intellectually fulfilled atheist. The same skeptic dismissed Paley's 'argument from design' by first stating that Paley had vastly understated the 'appearance of design' in biological systems. (Which is only fair, I suppose, since Paley penned his *Natural Theology* even before fellow Christian Louis Pasteur disproved spontaneous generation in 1859.) Every day that goes by, our knowledge and understanding of the great complexities involved in the genome and biochemistry makes the assertion that what appears to be designed isn't actually designed seem patently absurd to any fair minded, person. Today's skeptical community is hell-bent on showing that one of the observed iron laws of biology, biogenesis, can be broken, given enough time.

The evidence increasingly and progressively shows that it *cannot* and there is *no hope* for it *ever* being shown, because *the thing is not possible*. Simply stated, it is not about probabilities, but possibilities. That which is not possible will not be possible no matter how much time is allowed. That which is probable, given enough time, theoretically will happen eventually. (Or so goes the argument.) Our knowledge of biology increasingly shows that what we are dealing with is not in the category of probabilities, but possibilities.

Some wag once said that they would not accept that the genome is actually designed until they see written in the genome something like, "God was here." Given what we already know about both mankind and the clear witness of the genome, we may pray that God does not actually do such a thing—for our sake. Still, we can get a glimpse of the great hardening of the heart that is in progress even as we speak when we hear the same people demand such unequivocal examples of design within the genome, even as they proceed to insist that it is not actually possible to reliably detect design with the genome. With such an attitude, we can be certain that, in the first place, even if God did write such a message in the genome, they would likely not even see it and, in the second place, if they did, they would in willful defiance choose not to give that message its proper significance. In my opinion, they would instead claim that scientific evidence of 'directed panspermia' had finally been uncovered; that is, they would appeal to space aliens.

Incredible discoveries are being made that show that sometimes genetic instructions are written three-dimensionally, with the genome folding over on top of itself to read a message 'vertically' as well as 'horizontally.' In other words, we may assume that even the most hard core cynic is willing to accept that the essay you are presently reading is the product of an intelligent designer, but imagine how profoundly convinced you would be if you folded it in half and in half again and found that you could read an entirely different message with the words stacked one on top of the other. In that case, no one would dream of suggesting that this essay was generated by random movements of matter in space and time. The genome is incalculably more complex than this essay, and now we know that there is genuine information in it when read sideways or folded on top of itself and read vertically. Amazingly, the message than carries out its own instructions!

With such discoveries, there will be less and less room for doubt that life is the product of a designer with abilities far surpassing anything that could be expected from even the host highly advanced technological society... that is to say, at some point—I predict—something will be discovered where everyone agrees the plainest and most self-evident conclusion will be that the observed complexity simply is not possible according to the very laws of nature—and yet, there it is! At that point, the die will be cast for many people.

Indeed, it can be argued that this has already happened. The many people over the last century or so who have remained skeptical of the assertion that clearly designed things are only 'apparently designed' testifies to the fact that this threshold has already been met in many instances. In fact, in response to the genetic folding discussed above, one skeptic complained, "The creationists are going to love this. ... This is going to make my life very complicated." [15]

Or, it could get very simple, simply by surrendering to the plain implications of what is observed.

The above is an outline of some of the 'natural revelation' that could progressively strip away reasonable doubt regarding God as Christians understand Him, but there is another area where that is ripe for this pattern to unfold.

The Christian Scriptures, otherwise known as 'the Bible,' is often held in contempt, and its assertions regarding real history is one area that gets hostile treatment. This is odd, since every year that goes by more evidence surfaces that shows this history is accurate. From cities lost to history that are found right where the Bible says they would be to corroboration of the existence of historical persons thought to be scribal inventions (eg, Sennacharib, King David, and Pontius Pilate), the pattern is clear: given enough time, resources, and 'luck,' much, if not all, of the Bible will eventually be proved by archeological and manuscript discoveries. The argument can be made that this has already been sufficiently accomplished, and to refuse to grant this fact by some precisely illustrates the 'hardening of the heart' that has been discussed in this essay.

My prediction is that these discoveries will continue, and their importance will get progressively more significant. There are, in particular, two discoveries waiting to happen, which, in my opinion, would signal the impending second coming of Jesus representing the 'third great intrusion.' If either or both of these discoveries are made, *watch out*.

---

[15] He was then lambasted by his fellows for giving 'ammunition' to young-earth creationists.

It should go without saying that 'impending' is a relative term. If there is a characteristic of God that is evident if the substance of this essay be true, it is that He is patient.

Those two discoveries would be the conclusive discovery of Noah's Ark and the lost Ark of the Covenant—especially if the latter included two stone tablets, a jar of sweet bread, and a staff that still has its bud!

Leading up to these discoveries, there could be some other ones that would also be of great significance, such as the discovery of the chariots of the Egyptians who were swallowed up by the waters as they chased the Israelites out of Egypt, or of any of the numerous documents that the Bible occasionally refers to. For example, the writer of the Gospel of Luke, in the first few verses of the account explicitly references other accounts of Jesus' life, death, and resurrection. It is possible this is a reference to the other 'Gospels' we already know about but it is equally possible that there were other written accounts that haven't yet seen the light of day. There are other ancient history books that are referred to by some of the writers of the Old Testament. We may yet see some 'secular' accounts surface that have amazing implications. For example, at present Tacitus attests to the existence of Jesus and asserts that he was put to death by Pontius Pilate, but the time period of his *Annals* that actually covers the time in question is lost. Someday, it may be found, and what will it say?

There is also a third, very real discovery that could be made that ought to have a similar effect: the absolute determination that abiogenesis could not have happened without the help of an extremely intelligent agent. However, I personally do not think that if such a discovery was ever made, atheistic scientists would even recognize it, or, if they did, tell the rest of us about it. Just as the Pharisees decided to kill Jesus after they learned that he had raised Lazarus from the dead, the scientists would do all in their power to suppress knowledge of such a discovery.

I now rise to answer the specific question this essay was to address: why, in a world created and sustained by an all-powerful and good God, is there suffering in the world?

If I have prepared the groundwork sufficiently, the line of reasoning will come to one's mind quite naturally: if God were to intervene to prevent suffering, this very well could entail the complete and utter loss of innumerable individuals who, brought to the ultimate conviction that God exists, decided nonetheless that they would prefer to remain forever a rebel.

It might be objected, "But if there were no suffering, there would be no grounds for rebellion!"

This objection might be sincerely stated, but from my experience, there would still be those who would find cause to remain a rebel. There is in Christian theism, after all, much that many find objectionable, not just the existence of suffering.

For example, Christian theism insists that people were created in God's image, male and female, with monogamous relations "till death do they part." Many people, however, wish to have sex as often as they want, with as many people as they want, with a person of any gender as they please, with as little consequence as possible, and certainly without any guilt or pang of conscience. Of course, Christian theism contains no prohibition on having sex as often as you like. After all, God is the one who made humans 'male and female.' Sex was His creation.

The issue of sex and sexuality helps us understand the question of 'suffering' more accurately, or at least, more honestly.

Does the reader realize just how much suffering in the world actually derives from the human desire to have *laissez-faire* sexual activity? Millions of people end up with sexually transmitted diseases. There are millions of unwanted children that result, and millions of these are murdered. Despite assurances that abortion only kills a tiny clump of cells and that it is quite alright to "do it like they do it on Discovery Channel" and that STDs can be prevented by wearing condoms, or, at any rate, treated with drugs, the average person cannot shake the feeling that something about all this is just not quite right... the price for 'sex on demand' seems to cost more than the purveyors of it suggest. This is to be expected when conscience is the product of our design by God, and not a happenstance result of eons of development.

To put it bluntly, much of the suffering in the world in regards to human sexuality is Man's fault, *not God's*. Those who abstain until their wedding day need not fear sexually transmitted diseases. Those who wait to have sex until they are mature enough to bear the consequences, and understand that one of those consequences—having children—is part of the intrinsic package of what 'sex' is about, will not usually have to worry about 'unwanted' children.

Similarly, Christian theism puts limits on greedy materialism. Of all the theistic systems, Christianity is one of the few to embrace the actual goodness of the 'material.' It was gnosticism, *a heresy*, that said that the physical world was an illusion or worse, an evil foe of the 'spiritual.' Christianity, on the other hand, upheld the assertion made in Genesis that the universe God created, and all that was in it, was originally 'good.' From this it necessarily follows that the work of our hands and the sensual gifts we enjoy are actually things God intended for us.

Despite this, the Apostle Paul declared, "Everything is good, but not everything is beneficial." Or, in another place, "Do not become a slave to..." And let us not forget, "the root of all kinds of evil..."

Christian theism enjoins us to enjoy and make use of the material world, but within certain boundaries. We may not lie, cheat, steal, and kill to make a living or shore up our profits. This is a message that some people do not want to hear. Just as *for the Christian* sexuality does not rest on a *laissez-faire* basis, neither do our economic pursuits.[16]

How much of the suffering we witness every day in our world is the result of the greed, indifference, belligerence, and even laziness of Man himself? If a rich man eats a feast in front of a poor man who is poor and hungry for no fault of his own, is it God's fault that the poor man has no food? If one man steals the food from another, is it God's fault?

The Christian scriptures are packed full with condemnations of people abusing their authority and positions of power. Human arrogance added to great capabilities often leads to wicked, reprehensible actions, which are often painted in torrid detail, and usually accompanied with withering denunciations. Three examples leap to mind: King David, who killed the husband of Bathsheba so that he could cover up his adulterous affair with her; Nebuchadnezzar, who had difficulty understanding that he was not actually a god; King Herod, who bristled when John the Baptist condemned Herod's own adulterous and murderous behaviors, and so had John the Baptist imprisoned and ultimately beheaded. Powerful people usually don't like being told that they have limits and they certainly don't like the idea that their authority derives from God. They like to think there is something special about them that justifies whatever they happen to decide. And I haven't even mentioned what people will sometimes do to attain power in the first place.

How much of the suffering we see is the result of powerful and ambitious people trampling upon their fellow

---

[16] At this point, someone undoubtedly will begin thinking that we should endeavor to enforce these boundaries in secular society, such as within the laws of the land. While I will not repudiate that perspective totally, I also will not embrace it totally. It does not follow that the passages and principles described above, which pertain specifically to the Christian individual. There is no *warrant in these passages* for extending these principles to our governance. It is not to say that they can or cannot be so extended, only that if so, or if not, it will have to be justified on some other basis. In any case, that question is for an entirely different essay.

man and using their authority to further their own selfish aims rather than put that authority into service to the people they have authority over? Human history is virtually a seamless account of one abuse of power after another, and the consequences that followed. If one man crushes another man in the exercising of his authority, is it God's fault?

We could spin these scenarios endlessly, and the final step in the logic will lead us to the unanswerable question of why God allowed people to disobey him in the first place. Presumably, 'free will' was the reason, and the cost, though high, was one that God deemed worth it. For most of the steps beyond that, however, *Man* is culpable for the suffering. God's 'crime' is creating us in the first place. The proper question is not "Why is there suffering?" because the lion's share of that suffering is the result of humanity's action. The real question is, "Why did God create us *at all*, knowing that there would be suffering?"

Some would say it is better to not exist then to exist in a world where suffering exists. For example, 'ethicist' Peter Singer has urged that the entire human race sterilize itself specifically in order to create a world where suffering does not exist.[17] On this view, all of humanity should declare, with Job, "It is better to have not been born," and we should endeavor to actually make it so that no one else is actually born!

On the same view, however, one wonders if the more logical step is not to sterilize the whole human race, but rather to destroy it where it stands! According to Singer (and I paraphrase), "if we could see our lives...it would suck" but it is hard to see why this should be any different after being sterilized than before being sterilized. If it is better to not have existed rather than suffer, then it is better to not continue existing, too. At the least, in light of the suffering

---

[17] For some reason, he does not go further and apply the same argument to animal suffering—shouldn't we sterilize every organism on the planet that we believe has the ability to suffer?

we are experiencing or bound to experience, we would better off committing suicide and being done with it.

Singer, naturally, does not advocate for this. In fact, for as bad as suffering is, very few people think it is so bad that we should end our own lives and the lives of the human race. In the main, despite having lives that Singer suggests "is worse than we really think' we still choose to keep living.

Is it then, really a 'crime' that God even created us, even though He knew (much more intimately than we ever will!) just how much suffering would follow? If we say 'yes' then at logic's end we should be concluding that there is no reason to keep existing. Yet, most of us continue to exist and if people begin talking about ending their lives, we tend to think that is a sign that a person might be mentally ill—not fully rational and logical. Thus, by continuing to exist, and moreover, by not daily weighing our own suicide, we testify to the fact that, logic aside, the joys of existence generally outweigh the troubles of life. Or, to put it plainly: on balance, we cannot blame God for creating us, even though human history is packed with horrible suffering.

It is not too difficult to put the intuitive argument above on a sound, logical basis. It is a fact that most people are constantly engaged in what God is 'accused' of doing. Men and women continue to bring children into the world knowing full well that their child will almost certainly experience at least as much heartache as their parents do. We build cars and drive them around, even though we know that there will some who experience tremendous suffering on account of car accidents. We build houses even though they sometimes burn down. We eat food, even though we know that it is occasionally tainted. We use knives to cut our steak, even though we know it is possible we might slice ourselves. Or... someone may pick up a knife to kill another person with it. Or... someone may purposely burn down a house in order to kill the occupants (or collect the insurance). Or, someone might drive drunk, or worse, purposely drive into a crowd of people, killing some.

Yet, if we did not have knives, no one would be killed by a knife. If we did not eat, no one would die of food poisoning. If we did not have houses, no houses could burn down. If we did not drive, we could not die in car accidents. If we did not bring children into the world, there would be no more humans who could suffer and die. Are we therefore wicked and full of guilt if we provide the means by which suffering is mediated?

Why not? Because God created the means by which we create means by which suffering is mediated? Nonsense! In the list above, except for the eating of food part, it is *our* choice to have children, drive cars, build houses, distill alcohol, and establish insurance companies. Nowhere is it written in any divine book that humans must do these things. They are products of our own volition. Our own volition or not, no one (except perhaps Peter Singer) believes that merely having made them and created the conditions through which suffering could result has made us *culpable* for that suffering.

Two questions remain. First of all, the question will immediately rise, "Even so, surely God could intervene..." The entire first part of this essay was devoted to explain why God *could* intervene, but cannot—*if* He also wants genuine relationships with humans. At least, not until the opportune time. Secondly, we ask, "Well then, what about the suffering that is not caused through human volitions, such as accidents where no human agency is involved, like people dying in a volcanic eruption, or by disease?"

In the main, this second question is answered by the same answer offered for our first question. The difference is that in this second question, we cannot place culpability on Mankind's back, presumably leaving only God to shoulder the blame.

Unfortunately (for that argument), even here we must remember that within the traditional framework of Christian theism, there would be no death at all if not for the act of disobedience of the first man and woman. While it is hard to put our heads around it, Paul writes that all of creation was brought under punishment because of that act of disobedience. There wouldn't even be *accidental* deaths if Adam and Eve hadn't sinned. Disease would be unheard of.

Of course, many people, including many Christians, have dispensed with the idea that there really was an Adam and Eve. Still, most of those Christians would still affirm Paul's assertion that creation itself suffers from Man's sin, because they still (though not always) affirm Paul. These Christians may answer the question differently, but on this point, at least, it would be agreed that even much of the suffering and death that doesn't appear to be human-caused, turns out on further analysis to derive from humans after all.

We need not impugn their character in order to still see how it may be a human's fault that they suffered or died. For example, a person who dies from a volcanic eruption could have lived further away. A person who dies in a flood could have lived on high ground. A person who is destroyed by a tornado could have lived in a bunker underground. Indeed, we all could live in bunkers underground! If we die because an earthquake buries us in our bunker, well, we could have lived instead on high ground, no? For the most part, everyone understands that there are certain risks they are taking by being *anywhere*.

Few maintain that if God *really* loved us, he would have packed us into flame retardant, sterile Styrofoam balls that only allowed us to communicate telepathically.

Once we've really eliminated human culpability, there actually remain very few categories of suffering that we can put firmly at God's feet. There certainly aren't enough to get excited about, acting as though we've come up with a good reason to think God isn't good, or that he doesn't exist, or isn't worthy of our devotion. It all boils down to one very simple question: is it better to have loved and lost, rather than to have never loved at all?

God has answered that in the affirmative. By continuing to live our lives, loving and losing frequently and often, we testify to the fact that we *also* answer that in the affirmative.

Very few categories might remain, but the ones that do sorely prick us. As bad as it is to think about people who have suffered and died because of diseases or vast multitudes thrown into ovens, it is even worse when we are talking about very young people enduring such horrors. There will remain instances where even if we conceded the human element we find it unimaginable that a loving being with the capability to intervene would choose not to.

It is certainly not the purpose of this essay to minimize the pain and anguish that is often associated with suffering. It is good and proper that we are dismayed by the suffering in the world and that we seek to address it. Likewise, it is good and proper to wonder where God is in all this. The fallacy is in forgetting all of the other characteristics that God possesses, instead of focusing only on his omnipotence, omniscience, and omni-benevolence. As has already been explained, there is the matter of his transcendence and immanence, which entail certain, inescapable realities—even for an omnipotent, omniscient, and omni-benevolent being. The presumption is that God, thus described, would intervene in the way that we think He ought, which leads to the fallacy of concluding that since he does not so act, he must be quite indifferent to suffering.

In regards to God as the Christians understand him, that this presumption and the associated fallacy persist is ironic to say the least. Of all the worldviews out there that touch on the problem of suffering, it is Christianity that takes it the most serious.

For example, there are some worldviews out there that take suffering and death seriously, but ultimately regard it as somehow a self-created illusion. Buddhism and forms of gnosticism come to mind. In Hinduism, death is welcome— provided you are on your way to becoming one with the universe. Even on a view stripped of religious content (supposedly), death has a good and proper place in this world: on an evolutionary account, it is precisely because of the death (and presumably, all of the suffering that is usually associated with death) of countless numbers of organisms that I am even here to pen this essay, and you here to read it. Utilitarians take suffering so seriously that they will happily kill you to put you out of their misery, inevitably creating far more suffering than they alleviated, but at any rate death is seen as a release, not a horror.

Christianity categorically sees death as an enemy, indeed, the very last enemy to be overthrown (1 Corinthians 15:26). Suffering, too, is recognized as a great evil, but the answer the Scriptures give is not intellectual. What we see instead is God coming to the earth *personally* to suffer *with* and *alongside* us.

God is not indifferent. He understands that there are things worse than death *and* worse than suffering. For example, our eternal damnation. There *will* be a reckoning, but at the right time and in the right way, with an eye towards rescuing as many as can be saved.

He plays the long game. He very well could intervene in every case, and there would be short term advantages to this. However, by playing for short term gains, he would be giving up the possibility of something that can be gained only on a long term strategy. Like a general forced to give up one battle so that he can win the war, God endures all of the calamities that we do (and far more intimately than we ever could conceive or imagine) in order to win the final prize.

After pointing to the 'heroes of the faith,' many of whom died horrific deaths, the author of Hebrews encourages believers to look "to Jesus, the founder and perfecter of our faith, who for the joy that was set before him endured the cross, despising the shame, and is seated at the right hand of the throne of God."Jesus is put forth as the ultimate model, the one whom the 'heroes of the faith' were themselves imitators. *He* suffered pain and indignity. And why? The author tells us: "for the joy that was set before him."

And just what is that joy? You don't know? You haven't

figured it out yet?

Us.

It would take another essay the length of this one to expound on the concept of 'joy.' In some ways, that essay is more important than this one! For our purposes, though, I wish to ram home this critical thing about joy: it is categorically and substantially more consuming than suffering. It is not like the utilitarian's meager concept of 'happiness,' which is fleeting and shallow, the kind of thing that can be mimicked by drugs or fast living. On a view that sees the 'pleasure principle' as the highest aim for our life, it is clear that in the scales, suffering weighs much heavier. A moment of pleasure is not enough to outweigh a lifetime of suffering.

But joy is not like that. Joy is not something that is experienced, *per se*. It is a pervasive reality that transcends our existence and our experience of reality but is also immanent within it, such that we only occasionally *glimpse* it in all of its glory. A moment's glimpse of *joy* really does outweigh a great deal of suffering.

Happiness and suffering may be seen as being on the same sliding scale, but joy is something Other altogether.

We taste this joy on occasions in our lives with each other, and this is why we persist in making friends, marrying, eating and drinking, and begetting. It is why we tolerate the lows in life. Indeed, sometimes it is only because of these lows that we appreciate just how substantially different joy is from 'happiness.' We put up with the inevitable sufferings because beneath it all we see Something better. This, I call joy, and it, too, is one of the omni-characteristics of God himself.

It is for *this* reason that he tolerates suffering, and it is for *us* that *he* suffers.

For *Joy*.

When Apologetics is Not Welcome in Your Church

I receive a handful of emails a year from people who are interested in apologetics, recognize its importance, but struggle to have it seen the same way in their local congregations. Many of these people find me through my ministry's online apologetics academy, which is specifically geared towards 'lay' apologists. It is very often the case that apologetics is a recent discovery of theirs that has profoundly helped them, and they are shocked that others do not have the same perspective. This is, of course, after they ponder why it took them this long to hear about apologetics in the first place.

Most of the time, the obstacle is simply a lack of enthusiasm. Occasionally, it is outright hostility. Sometimes a lack of enthusiasm, especially among the staff and clergy, is a mask for deeper opposition. It would be wise to have some deliberate conversations to determine what the real hindrance to apologetics within the congregation really is.

However, because of the nature of apologetics, there is no way to stop you from bringing your studies to bear, shy of locking the church doors and keeping you out. Apologetics does call to mind arguments and evidence and certain time-worn approaches to philosophical and theological issues, but more than that, apologetics engenders *an attitude and approach*. Some hall marks of the apologetically-minded person is an unwillingness to answer questions with "It's just a matter of faith" or, "Don't ask questions, kid. Doubt kills." When the apologetically-minded person is presented with a thorny issue, he does not shrug his shoulders and act as though there is no way to sort it out. He does not resign himself to ignorance and does not commend that ignorance as 'faith.' He gets out his books, he does some research, he looks at the relevant Scripture verses, he invests some time in critical thinking and bounces his ideas off of others who have the same attitude. Many times, what begins as a 'thorny' issue turns out to be easily resolves, as soon as facts and information is brought to bear.

As a case in point, when the movie *The Da Vinci Code* came out, many Christians wandered around in a daze, wondering how to reconcile the claims of the movie with their Christian faith. Those are the ones who took the claims seriously. Others dismissed it along the lines of "Well, that's why we have faith." The real travesty and crying shame is that *anyone at all* was flummoxed by the insinuations of the book, because even a cursory understanding of the history of the Christian church and how the Bible came to us is enough to deal a death blow to such wild-eyed conspiracy-mongering. A little knowledge quickly dispels the challenge the movie is said to represent, like the fog disappears on its own as soon as the sun comes up, just a smidgen.

There *will* be things that even the apologist walks away from scratching his head, but it will be much later in the process than many people often suppose.

This raises the important point that there are a great many things that interest the apologist that might not be strictly construed as 'apologetics.' Simply knowing the facts can count as 'apologetics.' Merely being aware that Jericho existed as a real city, and has been found, can be 'apologetics', if the person in front of you is insisting that the Scriptures are mythology, through and through. In short, any piece of information, evidence, or line of argument can count as 'apologetics' if the purpose of sharing it is to ground oneself or others in actual reality. For that is one of the core assumptions of apologetics: *Christianity is real*. Jesus was— and is—real. The events really happened, *in history*, not 'in faith.' Our faith is in a real God, in real promises made by Him that he really fulfilled in Christ... or really will fulfill.

This is an attitude, not a subject area.

Thus, there is no way to exclude 'apologetics' from the congregation unless you yourself are excluded from the congregation.

Hence, introducing 'apologetics' in your congregation

need not necessarily be limited to such offerings as an 'apologetics series' during the adult Bible study hour for a month. If you teach a Sunday School class and you are apologetically minded, you will be doing 'apologetics' throughout the year, because your mindset and learning will be informing your lessons each and every Sunday.

Since more things count as 'apologetics' than one might normally think, you can also bring apologetics into the congregation without ever using the word. For example, instead of offering to do a four part series on apologetics, instead offer to do a study in the geography of Palestine. In the course of that four week study, you will ground the events described in the Scriptures in a real location that has a real history. You will orient people, so that they know that Jerusalem (for example) is a certain distance from Bethlehem which is a certain distance from the Sea of Galilee; in many minds, this is all 'old myth' and the cities just run together in their heads. The fact that people couldn't hop into their cars but had to walk these distances will add new perspective to the yearly trip to Jerusalem to attend the Passover- and since we mentioned it, let me tell you a word about the Passover and what that meant to the Jews at the time. You see how it works. Naturally, you'd also include some mention of interesting archeological finds that corroborate, substantiate, or even conclusively show (to the reasonable man) certain claims of Christianity are true... (for example, the Pilate Inscription.)

We tend to think of the whole work of the congregation in terms of the service, Bible studies, and youth group activities. 'Breaking in' on these functions may be difficult, because they require some consent and/or approval from the pastor, or a committee or board, or something similar. It may not be opposition to apologetics, per se. There may be enough volunteers (ha!) or the schedule might be all filled up. But these sorts of things are not the whole work of the Church.

I would argue that every man and woman's chief ministry

is to their own family. If you are 'apologetically minded,' you won't wait for the Sunday School teacher to get around to presenting some of the lines of evidence for the (real) resurrection of Christ. You'll be doing it yourself. It may not have occurred to you that this is 'doing apologetics in the church' but it certainly is.

More to the point, the spiritual leaders of every family in the Church are, biblically, the parents in those families. Not the pastor, not the DCE, or youth director, or even you, the 'official' apologist. In your desire to bring apologetics into your congregation, you may wish to consider that the perspective you bring in your conversations in the narthex, at the potluck, or whatever, counts equally as 'doing apologetics,' and indeed can have as much impact (or more, obviously) as a Sunday morning 'apologetics' presentation. You can of course mention in those conversations your belief that as parents we have an obligation to transmit the faith to our children in a robust manner, and hey, aren't you a parent? but you don't need to be as direct as that. You can convey the *attitude and approach* that apologetics study engenders by the comments you make, the books you recommend, and the points you emphasize.

To my knowledge, there is no church in America that requires committee approval for having conversations in the church foyer where you just 'happen' to mention the newest book by Gary Habermas or the fact that William Lane Craig is speaking nearby that weekend ("Oh, you don't know who William Lane Craig is? Let's do lunch tomorrow and I'll bring you up to speed.")

In my years of apologetics experience, I have found that the little conversations turn out to have the biggest impacts, often without knowing about it. I recently had a phone call with someone who wanted to talk to me about something I said to him almost *ten years earlier* on the bleachers at a track meet.

Many people reading this may agree that what I have described sounds all well and good, but it doesn't quite seem satisfying. Doing really important work in apologetics surely means having your congregation view you as an authority on such things, or at least get you to speak on things on occasion, right? Surely it means snagging a debate with the local atheist at area community college? That is, don't we feel that if we're doing serious apologetics work, we'd be taken seriously? I admit, I have felt the same way. I cannot speak for everyone, but I suspect, if you are like me, this sentiment comes more from a certain kind of pride—and not the good kind. I suspect, when I feel this way, that it boils down to the simple sin of coveting, where I covet the apparent 'success' of other apologists.

But that just goes to show you why we need to distrust our feelings and 'take every thought captive for Christ' because I know intellectually that when the chips are down, what really counts and what really matters are the souls of our fellow man. That is the sort of thing that I wouldn't let a little congregational apathy on the subject of apologetics get in the way of. Nor should we let grandiose visions of ourselves, boldly contending for the faith, prevent us from seeing and acting on the multitude of small but important opportunities to strengthen the faith of our fellow Christians or whittle away at objections of non-Christians.

And for many of us, there will remain after everything else, our very own children. Wouldn't that be enough warrant, all on its own?

IN DEFENSE OF 'LUTHERAN' BAPTISM

A couple of years ago there was a local radio program that hosted a debate between an area ELCA (Lutheran) bishop and the pastor of an area Evangelical congregation on the subject of baptism, infant baptism in particular. The Lutheran defense was embarrassing to say the least. It amounted to little more than the assertion: "Infant baptism was the historic practice of the Church..." which may very well be verbatim. The evangelical retorted with Bible verses. This is usually a winning tactic in debates about what the Bible says! Infant baptism may indeed be the historic practice of the church but that can't be the sum of your argument.

What I intend to do in this essay is present one Lutheran's perspective on baptism. I do not want to say "*the* Lutheran understanding of baptism" for a variety of reasons. First of all, I'm not a theologian. Second of all, I don't wish to speak for all Lutherans. My view can definitely be called 'Lutheran' but I am sure other Lutherans may think differently on some points and they may be in a better position to speak for Lutheranism.

All that said, it would be too awkward to continually issue these caveats so when portraying my view I will say 'the Lutheran view...' instead of 'my view' or 'one particular Lutheran's view.'

Finally, it is a common academic approach to gather up and summarize all the viewpoints and reiterate past controversies and document developments on an issue over time until finally making one's own arguments and observations. In the case of baptism (among others) I think that approach is actually part of the problem in understanding Lutheran baptism. That kind of approach descends into a battle of proof texts but the real difference in viewpoints here stems from the fact that Lutherans have an entirely different foundation of thought that undergirds their view on Baptism than Evangelicals do. This is obscured in

Battles of Bible Verses.

Similarly, the constant countering of objections posed by other viewpoints forgets the fact that when verses are produced in support of a position, they are done so in light of the foregoing assumptions and understandings of the belief. In some cases, it would be pointless to make a particular objection because the objection stems first from the belief that your particular perspective is right: but whether or not that perspective is right is precisely what is up for debate! So, my goal here is to issue a 'positive' treatment on baptism that is not to be understood for what it is against, but what it is for.

No one should presume to think that I am issuing forth an academic work. I am stating what I believe in the best way I know how. I will only occasionally as seems necessary—and even then only reluctantly—engage objections that I have often heard to the Lutheran understanding of baptism.

I am certainly not interested in countering the objections of atheists and secular humanists, for obviously I do not share their anti-supernaturalistic bias.

PART ONE

What was the old testament? A testament is an agreement between two parties. What we call the 'Old Testament' covers much more than God's agreement with the Israelites, though of course that is a substantial portion of it. Another important aspect of the 'old testament' is that it represents the early unfolding of God's overall plan of saving all of humanity, not limiting God's grace to the Jews. This plan culminated in His personal appearance as Jesus of Nazareth to accomplish what no sinful man could accomplish. This established a new covenant between two parties: God and All Mankind, and in particular, the Church.

The covenant that God made with the Israelites when being led by Moses was instituted with fire and brimstone. It came to be called, in shorthand, 'the law of Moses.' Many more things are included in this, however. For example, God instituted the ceremonial law with Moses on account of the fact that God was going to actually dwell with the Israelites in the tabernacle and eventually the temple in Jerusalem. It is easy for moderns to underestimate the significance of this covenant because we tend to buy into the subtle anti-supernaturalism of our age.

What I mean is this: as the story goes, God led the Israelites out of Egypt with signs and wonders that were unparalleled in human history and *visibly* led them as a pillar of cloud by day and of fire by night (Ex. 13:21-22), putting to shame the 'gods' of the Egyptians and Canaanites. As far as I can tell, God's presence remained visibly with the Israelites for generations upon generations. The book of Exodus ends with these words:

> Then the cloud covered the tent of meeting, and the glory of the LORD filled the tabernacle. And Moses was not able to enter the tent of meeting because the cloud settled on it, and the glory of the LORD filled the tabernacle. Throughout all their journeys, whenever the cloud was taken up from over the tabernacle, the people of Israel would set out. But if the cloud was not taken up, then they did not set out till the day that it was taken up. For the cloud of the LORD was on the tabernacle by day, and fire was in it by night, in the sight of all the house of Israel throughout all their journeys.

Seemingly, the glory of the LORD was present in some visible fashion until at last Solomon finished construction of the temple in Jerusalem and we read in 1 Kings 8:

> And when the priests came out of the Holy Place, a cloud filled the house of the LORD, so that the priests could not stand to minister because of the cloud, for the glory of the LORD filled the house of the LORD.

This is the story, but I suspect that moderns—even Christians—tend to gloss over these events as though the Israelites had exaggerated natural phenomena or read into circumstances 'miracles' that perhaps we all have experienced at one time or another, but we 'know' were products of chance or coincidence. One might object that Christians would never discount such things. However, one often hears concerns about how hard God was on the Israelites for their disobedience and how aggressive God was in eliminating the Canaanites... but God's harsh treatment of them is more than accounted for by the realization that given he was immediately present to the senses to the entire region, they obviously had no excuses for their behavior. Atheists constantly demand such overwhelming evidence of God's existence... they might want to consider the fate of those who once had exactly that... and still refused to submit.

What does all of this have to do with baptism? What I'm driving at is that the old covenant was not some skimpy spiritual insight from a charismatic leader who managed to bamboozle his way out of captivity through clever diplomacy. The old covenant was established with power in full sight of the Egyptians and Israelites and well within corroboration for the Canaanites. It was not the kind of thing to dispense with easily. The Jews can be forgiven their stubbornness over the centuries as they strove against the Romans and false gods because it was within the memory of their people that God had once dwelled among them *visibly and in power*.

In light of this, the skepticism with which Jesus was greeted by contemporary Jews is understandable and to a degree it was even warranted... until Jesus began performing his great works.

Consider the significance of Jesus' claim that he, *himself*, had come to fulfill the law (Matthew 5:17). When Jesus responds to the high priest of a people who had witnessed the full might of the LORD, "In the future you will see the Son of Man sitting at the right hand of the Mighty One and coming on the clouds of heaven," we well understand the charge of blasphemy... unless, of course Jesus is the only one who could make such a statement truthfully.

The old covenant was an amazing thing. It was an agreement between God and one small nation on earth whereby God agreed to live among them in a visible, powerful way, with certain conditions. It was not the sort of thing to be treated lightly. Now consider what the author of the book of Hebrews says about it in 10:1: "... the law is but a shadow of the good things to come instead of the true form of these realities..."

I note in this passage that Hebrews does not say *an image* of the good things that are coming, but rather *a shadow*. Imagine, if you will, standing in front of a statue of a man. You can reach out and touch it and by drawing near you can examine it in increasing detail. Now if you snap a picture with your digital camera you'll have an image of the statue. You can learn a lot about the statue from examining the picture and can zoom in according to your resolution. There are limitations, though. For example, you cannot walk around behind the image. You can touch the image if you wanted but you would not feel the texture of the statue. Now let's say that the sun is hitting the statue and you examine the shadow that is cast behind it. You are left with a shape and outline which will yield very little information about the thing casting the shadow.

Now, the law, we are told, was like that shadow. The reality is more profound by many degrees. In comparison, even humans themselves are more wondrous since they were made in the image of God, not the shadow of God (whatever that would be).

The old covenant of the law, though marked with the fire and power of God, was still mere shadow in comparison with "the good things that are coming."

The book of Hebrews speaks extensively about the difference between the old covenant and the new covenant. The superiority of the latter over against the former is an important component of this discussion, but we are not going to cite full chapters of the book of Hebrews. We'll take just a handful of passages with a few emphases of my own:

For Jesus has been counted worthy of more glory than Moses—as much more glory as the builder of a house has more honor than the house itself. (3:3)

This makes Jesus the guarantor *of a better covenant*. (7:22)

For the law appoints men in their weakness as high priests, but the word of the oath, which came later than the law, appoints a Son who has been made perfect forever. (7:28)

They [the Levitical high priests] serve a copy and shadow of the heavenly things. For when Moses was about to erect the tent, he was instructed by God, saying, "See that you make everything according to the pattern that was shown you on the mountain." But as it is, Christ has obtained a ministry that *is as much more excellent* than the old as the covenant he mediates is better, since it is enacted *on better promises*. (8:5-6)

In speaking of a new covenant, he makes the first one obsolete. And what is becoming obsolete and growing old is ready to vanish away. (8:13)

But when Christ appeared as a high priest of the good things that have come, then through the *greater and more perfect* tent (not made with hands, that is, not of this creation)... (9:11)

Therefore, brothers, since we have confidence to enter the holy places by the blood of Jesus, *by the new and living way* that he opened for us through the curtain, that is, through his flesh, and since we have a great priest over the house of God, let us draw near with a true heart in full assurance of faith, with our hearts sprinkled clean from an evil conscience and *our bodies washed with pure water*. (10:19-22)

For you have not come to what may be touched, a blazing fire and darkness and gloom and a tempest and the sound of a trumpet and a voice whose words made the hearers beg that no further messages be spoken to them. ... But you have come to Mount Zion and to the city of the living God, the heavenly Jerusalem, and to innumerable angels in festal gathering, and to the assembly of the firstborn who are enrolled in heaven, and to God, the judge of all, and to the spirits of the righteous made perfect, and to Jesus, the mediator of a new covenant, and to the sprinkled blood that speaks *a better word* than the blood of Abel. (12:18-24)

The principle is clear: the new covenant is greater, better, superior, and more perfect than the old covenant. The old covenant is a shadow of the real thing that is recognized in the new covenant. What the old covenant was unable to do the new covenant accomplishes in spades. The new covenant is not simply a replacement of the old covenant, like one might trade in a horse for a bicycle. The old covenant is like a drawing of a Model T while the new covenant is a BMW. As such, it can do all the things the Model T could do but do it better, faster, and more efficiently. *All* the things in the old covenant are still there in the new covenant, but spiffed up and given radically new capabilities.

When we say 'new capabilities' we do not only mean new features and functions, but capabilities in new dimensions. The ability of an actual coffee cup to hold actual coffee is a higher-level capability than what an image of a coffee cup is able to do. Now imagine that the actual coffee cup that you consider to be a 'real' cup is itself only a shallow representation of a 'heavenly' cup. What might the 'heavenly' cup be able to do that even our own ceramic cups cannot do? At any rate, the New Covenant involves this kind of 'newness' along with some of the more conventional ideas of 'new' we might imagine.

This is an important biblical principle. It is also why so many of the first Christians were Jews. No one knew and understood the old covenant like the Jews did and so no one could understand the new covenant like a Jew could.

It follows from the foregoing that it would be absurd to maintain that there is any aspect of the new covenant that is *less* potent than that which it corresponds to in the old testament.

Before applying this to the question of baptism we must point out other components to how God works and how this relates to the supplanting of the old testament with the new testament.

It might help to perceive of God as an author and think about great human literature and then extrapolate from there, and then contend that whatever we see human authors do, God does, but does much better. This would be a fun exercise to engage in, highlighting plot elements such as conflict and climax and the like, but for my purposes what I want to detail are certain creative elements unique to God's operation in history.

For example, while God certainly could act arbitrarily and capriciously, in fact he acts justly and follows through on themes clean across the centuries. For an illustration of what I mean consider Jesus' statement in Matthew 5 that he has not come to abolish the law but to fulfill it. God does not abandon old themes, he fulfills them, harmonizes them, and repeats them with new colors.

There is a logic to the plot as it unfolds. Others have noticed various aspects of it such as God's narrowing of his plan of redemption through the Jews, then the tribe of Judah, then the family of David, then the town of Bethlehem until finally it was distilled down into one man, Immanuel. In the course of this he established a special relationship with the Israelites as we have noted but he was not indifferent to the affairs of the other nations and in fact in one case the unfolding had to wait a bit until after the sins of the Amorites had reached their full measure (Genesis 15:16). Despite God's association with the Israelites, it is clear that this isn't because the Jews were so noble and righteous but because he wanted to use them to reach the Gentiles. But the old promises and logic doesn't disappear. When Immanuel begins walking the planet he goes first and foremost to the Jews (see for example Matt. 15:21-28). The time for going to the gentiles would come later, after the children had received their bread.

The same sort of logic is in play when Paul writes to the Romans that the gospel "is the power of God for salvation to everyone who believes, to the Jew first and also to the Greek." Similarly, when Paul describes the coming of the Lord in his first book to the Thessalonians he says, "... the dead in Christ will rise first. *Then* we who are alive, who are left, will be caught up together with them." You see, each thing in turn, as is proper.

God's construction of his plan of salvation on the foundation of the people of Israel raises fascinating questions: Did God have to do it this way? Wouldn't it have been easier just to appear on earth and say, "Hey, I'm God!" and go from there? In fact, why even die as a sacrifice at all?

In defense of the sovereignty and omnipotence of God some go too far and contend that God could very well have done anything that he liked. Actually, some choices that we can *imagine* would likely have been against his very nature—which omnipotence doesn't permit, because asking God to go against his nature is to ask him to do the nonsensical. For whatever reason (and He knows the reasons better than we) he deemed that it was necessary to unfold the plan of salvation in this way and it was necessary that holy blood be shed in order to win the freedom of a fallen human race. We are talking here of the 'deep magic' that Aslan invokes in C.S. Lewis's *The Lion, the Witch, and the Wardrobe*.

Having returned to blood, we have returned to a comparison to the old and the new covenant. As is written in the book of Hebrews:

> But when Christ appeared as a high priest of the good things that have come, then through the greater and more perfect tent (not made with hands, that is, not of this creation) he entered once for all into the holy places, not by means of the blood of goats and calves but by means of his own blood, thus securing an eternal redemption. For if the blood of goats and bulls, and the sprinkling of defiled persons with the ashes of a heifer, sanctify for the purification of the flesh, how much more will the blood of Christ, who through the eternal Spirit offered himself without blemish to God, purify our conscience from dead works to serve the living God. (Heb. 9:11-14)

When the old covenant was established it was established in blood in the sacrificial system. The blood of animals could not redeem Man. That blood was a mere shadow and copy of the BLOOD that *could* redeem man. A picture of blood could not sustain a living creature the way that real blood can, but even real blood cannot atone for sins; for that you need even 'realer' blood.[18]

So now it must be re-iterated that this is not simple analogy or metaphor. There isn't something figurative about the power of Christ's blood to redeem... Christ's *actual* blood *really* does redeem. What the blood of goats and bulls symbolized, Christ's blood accomplished. It is *more real* than

---

[18] Found on the Internet: "If something is real, it can't be more than that. It can't be more real." The author of Hebrews would disagree strenuously.

their blood and thus is capable of accomplishing greater things.

This brings us to one more very important component of the old and new covenant. The old covenant of the law was of the flesh but the new covenant is of the spirit.

It is not uncommon to hear people—even Christians—talking about something spiritual as though it were ghostly, as though that which is fleshly had more substance than that which is spiritual. Nothing can be further than the truth. It is that which is unseen that is eternal, and the seen that will pass away (2 Cor. 4:18). It is the eternal that cannot be shaken and the temporal that can (Heb. 12:26-27).

Our state without the redemptive power of Christ's blood and the empowering of the Spirit is often called the 'Old Adam.' Here again the inclination is to view the fleshly 'Old Adam' as a metaphor or allegory but a plain reading of the New Testament reveals it to be much more.

Consider, for example, this passage from Romans 5:12-14

> Therefore, just as sin came into the world through one man, and death through sin, and so death spread to all men because all sinned—for sin indeed was in the world before the law was given, but sin is not counted where there is no law. Yet death reigned from Adam to Moses, even over those whose sinning was not like the transgression of Adam, *who was a type of the one who was to come.*

In this passage, we are told that Adam is a 'type' or 'pattern' of Jesus. However, we have established that 'patterns' are not meaningless symbols to God but 'plot elements' he uses and chooses to abide by as he unfolds the salvation story. When Paul proceeds to say, "because of one man's trespass, death reigned through that one man, " he is not kidding that death reigned *through* Adam in a literal, real way! The truth of it forms the basis for his confidence when he continues his sentence and concludes, how "*much more* will those who receive the abundance of grace and the free gift of righteousness reign in life through the one man Jesus Christ.." (Romans 5:17)

If you dismiss the reality of the former, there is no reason to ascribe reality to the latter. When he says that 'we all die in Adam,' Paul is appealing to a real truth that he expects his Jewish readers to acknowledge. If that part is not really true, then neither is the part about all being alive in Christ.

Paul employs the same logic in 1 Corinthians 15:20-24

But in fact Christ has been raised from the dead, the firstfruits of those who have fallen asleep. For as by a man came death, by a man has come also the resurrection of the dead. For *as in Adam all die, so also in Christ shall all be made alive*. But each in his own order: Christ the firstfruits, then at his coming those who belong to Christ. Then comes the end, when he delivers the kingdom to God the Father after destroying every rule and every authority and power.

The one who insists that it is mere metaphor that "in Adam all die" may as well conclude it is also mere metaphor that in Christ all will be made alive. Some Gospel that would be!

What does it mean to be 'in Adam'? The Scriptures provide numerous clues. For our purposes, I mean only to establish that there is a very real sense in which the old man really is in Adam somehow, just as the new man really is 'in Christ.' Not symbolically, but really.

There is some sort of organic relationship between Adam and the rest of us, though I do not here assert that I understand it very well. When God established the pattern for his plan for marriage in Genesis 2:24 where the pattern for biblical marriage is set forth, we are told that the men and the woman become one flesh: and God really means one flesh! God's purpose in this, according to Malachi 2:15 is so that godly offspring is the result. Somehow in the physical sexual act, though two people are witnessed to the eyes God confidently asserts there is but one flesh.

Again, not symbolically or in some cheap romantic sentiment, but really... otherwise it would make absolutely no sense when Paul protests, "Do you not know that your bodies are members of Christ? Shall I then take the members of Christ and make them members of a prostitute? Never! Or do you not know that he who is joined to a prostitute becomes one body with her?" (1 Cor 6:12-17) He then proceeds to cite the Genesis 2:24 passage and concludes, "But he who unites himself with the Lord is one with him in spirit."

But from the foregoing, it is known that my belief is that when it says we are one with the Lord in spirit we aren't talking about some vacuous sentiment, but rather insisting on some fundamental participation in the unseen and eternal realities. The spiritual is *more real* than the physical, not less. Always.

Since we all descend from Adam, we are all the manifestation of the 'one fleshness' that he experienced with Eve. Again, I do not mean to say I understand it only to assert that the Scriptures are clear that this is a definite reality. On account of this reality, Paul urges believing spouses to remain with their unbelieving spouses: "For the unbelieving husband is made holy because of his wife, and the unbelieving wife is made holy because of her husband. *Otherwise your children would be unclean, but as it is, they are holy*." (1 Cor 7:14)

The notion that a non-believing spouse and even children could somehow have sanctification imparted by virtue of the one flesh union is probably disturbing to some but Paul says what he says. And Paul does not stop here!

This may seem like a detour but in fact we are right on track. In Ephesians 5 the Apostle Paul explicitly makes use of this implicit understanding when he urges husbands to love their wives just as Christ loved the church. He says,

... husbands should love their wives as their own bodies. He who loves his wife loves himself. For no one ever hated his own flesh, but nourishes and cherishes it, just as Christ does the church, because we are members of his body. "Therefore a man shall leave his father and mother and hold fast to his wife, and the two shall become one flesh." This mystery is profound, and I am saying that it refers to Christ and the church.

God's use of patterns, with the new covenant exhibiting exponential new twists, should be clear. Husbands and wives *really do* become one flesh... they are one body. Just as literally, we are members of Christ's body, as we are His bride (Eph. 5:25). The pattern of temporal biblical marriage *is expanded upon* in regards to Christ and his Church. Just as the first man and wife gave birth to the temporal human race, and then spread death to it, The Heavenly Man and Wife give birth to spiritual beings and spread life.

This unity in Christ is crucial to understand for in many quarters this again is something that is treated as 'spiritual,' like an abstraction, and not an organic reality, albeit at an 'unseen' level. When Paul says that we are one in Christ, he really means it.

We could rattle off passage after passage to accentuate this concept but odds are that the reader is well aware of them. But does the reader believe what they read? If anyone wishes to engage in a study, I submit as simple examples 1 Cor. 13:12-29, Eph. 2:11-3:6, Phil. 3:7-11, Col. 3:3, and dozens of others you can stumble upon through a casual reading of the New Testament.

We are accustomed to reading variations on 'in Christ' in the New Testament but I submit that this is usually talking about something very real. Believing 'in' Christ is believing *into* him. *We are in Christ.*

It isn't arbitrary, either. There is a logic to it which is elucidated often in the Scriptures and is rarely treated in doctrinal texts. We are in Christ because it is by virtue of our union with Christ that we are saved. It is too simplistic to *only* say 'we are saved by grace through faith' because the Scriptures recount for us the process by which this salvation happens and it bears on the question of baptism.

The book of Colossians outlines this process, culminating in chapter 3:1-4:

> Since, then, you have been raised with Christ, set your hearts on things above, where Christ is seated at the right hand of God. Set your minds on things above, not on earthly things. *For you died, and your life is now hidden with Christ in God.* When Christ, who is your life, appears, then you also will appear with him in glory.

Here we see directly that we are in Christ, yes, *but first we died*. Now hidden in Christ, when Christ appears we appear with him.

Is this idea that we died a mere metaphor? If so, then it is also a metaphor that when Christ appears we appear with him in Glory.

When did we die? How did we die? At what point were we hidden with Christ?

This idea of 'death' as one of the stages of salvation runs through the book of Colossians and other books as well. This gritty element of salvation flies in the face of the template of euphoric altar calls and stirring decisions for Christ.

Death.

Somehow, we die and our life becomes hidden with Christ and this results in an eventual appearance in glory. Why?

We gain another clue from Colossians 2:13:

> When you were dead in your sins and in the uncircumcision of your sinful nature, *God made you alive with Christ*. He forgave us all our sins, having

canceled the written code, with its regulations, that was against us and that stood opposed to us; he took it away, *nailing it to the cross*. And having disarmed the powers and authorities, he made a public spectacle of them, *triumphing over them by the cross*.

This passage explains that our salvation consists in being made alive with Christ. When was Christ made alive? We know when he died; this passage reminds us twice. He died on the cross. The sterile analogizing mood that engages this passage will assume that this idea that God made us alive with Christ is another one of those 'spiritual' statements that issues forth in warm and fuzzies and nothing more. What if, however, Paul is describing something he believes is literally the case?

If so, then we begin to see a picture shaping up. We are raised in glory, with Christ, because we are present with him, and *in him*, in his death on the cross. Not figuratively, *but really*.

Can a clearer statement to this effect be found? Indeed, we find it in passages preceding the ones in Colossians we have already cited, namely in 2:9-12

For in Christ all the fullness of the Deity lives in bodily form, and you have been given fullness in Christ, who is the head over every power and authority. In him you were also circumcised, in the putting off of the sinful nature, not with a circumcision done by the hands of men but with the circumcision done by Christ, *having been buried with him* **in baptism** *and raised with him* through your faith in the power of God, who raised him from the dead.

Here we see in more detail that our salvation is obtained by our union with Christ's death and burial and then are also raised with him, as well.

Another passage that states this in clear language is Romans 6:3-11 which we will cite in full:

Or don't you know that all of us who were baptized *into Christ Jesus* **were baptized** *into his death*? We were therefore *buried with him* **through baptism** into death in order that, *just as Christ was raised from the dead* through the glory of the Father, *we too* may live a new life. *If we have been united with him like this in his death, we will certainly also be united with him in his resurrection.* For we know that our old self was crucified with him so that the body of sin might be done away with, that we should no longer be slaves to sin—because anyone who has died has been freed from sin.

Now, *if we died with Christ, we believe that we will also live with him.* For we know that since Christ was raised from the dead, he cannot die again; death no longer has mastery over him. The death he died, he died to sin once for all; but the life he lives he lives to God.

Here we have in verse 5 a straight-forward passage that explicitly lays out the logic: we are united with Christ in his death so that when he rises, we are with him in his new life. It would appear that the mechanism by which God saves us is by joining us with Christ on the cross so that when he was crucified, "our old self is crucified with him" and by virtue of our uniting in this way, we are present with Christ in his resurrection. God smuggles us through eternal peril by hiding us safe and securely inside... himself.

The astute reader will note that in both the Colossians passage and in the Romans passage it is stated precisely how God performs this smuggling act, and it is the subject of this essay: baptism.

We are not merely "buried with Christ' but ' buried with him *through baptism into death*" (Romans 6:4) and "having been buried with him *in baptism* and raised with him" (Colossians 2:12). Apparently, our uniting with Christ's death is achieved in and through baptism.

Some reading this treat all of this almost as if 'baptism' was intended by Paul to be used only for devotional value. On this view, these passages do not describe real spiritual events (where by 'spiritual' I mean something unseen, substantial, and eternal) but are just signs, pictures, and symbols. However, a plain reading of these two passages gives no indication that Paul is talking about mere symbolism. He is asserting the real method by which God saves a fallen race, and unfortunately for some, baptism therefore must be seen as one means by which this salvation is wrought.

Consider the objection made by some to this view of baptism. After citing this very passage, one theologian of this school explains, "Baptism in the New Testament is *a sign* of being born again, being cleansed from sin, and beginning the Christian life."

One is left scratching his head in amazement, wondering if we are reading the same text, for Romans 6:3 plainly says, and I repeat, "Or don't you know that all of us who were baptized into Christ Jesus were baptized into his death" and says nothing about baptism being a 'sign of being born again' or 'being cleansed from sin.' Certainly Romans 6 talks about sin being dealt with: by sticking it to the cross with nails, not by 'cleansing.' And certainly it marks the beginning of the Christian life, but not as some trite personal commitment whereby through our public declaration we single-handedly graft ourselves into the Church, but rather by virtue of our proximity in Christ's body as it shudders in death, drops into Hades like a comet, where then like new wine in old wine skins it bursts out of the tomb in power before ascending on high glory to sit down at the right hand of God.

According to this contrary view, when contemplating whether or not baptism does *anything*, the 'spiritual benefit' to believers is "the blessing of God's favor that comes with obedience, as well as the joy that comes through public professions of one's faith, and the reassurance of having a clear physical picture of dying and rising with Christ and of washing away sins."

This theologian would have saved us time if in answer to the question 'does baptism do anything?' he simply said, "No." For his idea of baptism is only a 'physical *picture* of dying and rising with Christ' (emphasis mine) but of course a picture of dying and rising with Christ is just that: only a picture. I for one would choose a real steak over a picture of one any day of the week but on this understanding there is no real steak, only pictures of them. Jesus said that man does not live by bread alone. Imagine how quickly we would starve if we had to suffice with only pictures of bread!

It would take a lot of time to get to the real root of such objections, but we can tackle the most immediate fallacy quickly enough. In his own comparing and contrasting of the old and new covenant *vis a vis* baptism, he admits that baptism is the new covenant form of old covenant circumcision. The Colossians passage mentioned above clearly links circumcision with baptism, so this far so good. But then he explains,

> ...in the new covenant it is appropriate that infants *not* be baptized, and that baptism only be given to those who give evidence of genuine saving faith, because membership in the church is based on an internal spiritual reality, not on physical descent.

Never mind the reference to baptizing infants. Note instead that on this view it is entirely forgotten that in the old covenant, there was a way in which young males could *literally* be included in the people of Israel but on this view, the new covenant replacement to circumcision, baptism, accomplishes *literally nothing*. Everything that needed to be done, on his view, is already done before the baptism takes place.

It is not intended here to make a detour into arguing for baptism of infants. This is a logical consequence of the view I am detailing, but that isn't the point. The point is that baptism is the new covenant replacement for circumcision and as such, if in fact the old covenant is a shadow and the new covenant the (much higher) reality, baptism will not do *less* than what circumcision did, but will profoundly do much more!

A full discussion on Christian baptism would require here a full discussion on old testament circumcision, for circumcision would provide for us the general outlines and vague notion of what baptism does with detail and clarity. For the sake of time we will omit that full study except for making some general points.

Old testament circumcision was required by God of anyone who would be part of the nation of Israel. 'Membership' required it, and it wasn't optional. It was required also of males 8 days old. Females were not circumcised, but even males who were not Jewish but captured slaves had to be circumcised. Very likely, even circumcision wasn't 'just' a sign, either, or else God wouldn't have hunted Moses down in order to kill him for not circumcising his son (Ex. 4:24-26), but I digress.

If we hadn't had Paul's statements in Colossians and Romans and elsewhere to the effect that baptism went above and beyond what circumcision did, we could have still deduced that something existed that replaced circumcision. Just about every other aspect of the Old Testament is mirrored and expanded on in this way- Adam/Jesus, Sacrifice of Animals/Sacrifice of Jesus, etc, etc. Of course, it helps when Paul spells it out as clearly as he does, especially in the Romans 6 passage.

What we've really boiled the discussion down to two elementary questions: First, "What *is* baptism?" Secondly, "What does it mean to be saved?"

The passages that speak to baptism speak to both questions. To answer the first question, we would turn to the clearest description of what baptism is and what it does, and this is laid out in explicit terms in Romans 6, and pretty clearly also in Colossians 2, and more ambiguously in 1 Peter 3:21 which does at least say precisely *how* baptism saves: "It saves by the resurrection of Jesus Christ."

God saves us by placing us into Jesus so that we can share in his resurrection. What does it mean to be saved? It means to be present, really, in the very body of Jesus as he dies and rises from the grave. It just so happens that baptism is one way in which God 'puts' people into Jesus.

Baptism is the literal union with Christ in his death so that it can be said that if we have died with him we surely rose with him.

It is accomplished by the power of God, not the declaration of man. The water in baptism is *both* a visible 'sign' of a real transformation and a means by which God effects a real transformation.

Having established the theoretical framework for understanding Biblical Lutheran baptism, it is time to delve deeper into some discrete areas of application... and controversy.

PART TWO

One of the chief objections that will be raised to this understanding of baptism is that the new covenant is one in which there is "*one* mediator between God and men, the man Christ Jesus" (1 Timothy 2:5). A baptism that *really does* bury us with Christ, performed by 'the hands of men' (Col 2:11) seems to be out of tune with the idea that in the new covenant we are born of God... "not of blood nor of the will of the flesh nor of the will of man..." (John 1:13). Add in the idea that people can be baptized ('by the hands of men'?) before they've even said their first word and it becomes difficult to make sense of things.

In point of fact, upon discovering that baptism is the 'new' circumcision (Col 2), we should see that such ideas are not out of tune, they are to be expected. Baptism *should be* similar in form, even as it is tremendously more potent.

I propose that the real difficulty here has little to do with the fact that people are involved in baptism than it does with the idea that people are involved *at all, in anything*. To these objections we can lodge our own, like, "Why send out disciples to preach the Gospel to all nations? Why not just provide special revelation to distant continents? If there is no mediator between God and man, what is the point of evangelism? Why should tiny tribes on isolated islands be eternally punished just because Christian missionaries haven't gotten there yet? Why rely on fallible time-bound humans who even after they arrive at said islands do as much damage as they do good?" Or, to top it off, "Why have humans circumcise male children eight days old when all God has to do to include a person in the promises of the old covenant with Israel is *declare* it?"

Indeed, many people in the quest for consistency have taken these questions to heart and have essentially agreed: since God has predestined some before the beginning of the world, evangelism isn't necessary, Gospel proclamation isn't necessary, Christian education isn't necessary, and so on and so forth. But there is a problem: these things appear to be commanded. What is commanded is necessary, obviously. The solution put forward: these things are not done because they actually achieve anything but simply out of obedience to the Word. In short, we do them because they have devotional value to the individual.

Now, this might seem absurd but I want to be clear that I have actually heard such things from people. For example, in one discussion a young man explicitly stated that free will is an illusion and God 'has mercy on whom he wants to have mercy and he hardens whom he wants to harden' (Romans 9:17). I asked him then why he was so involved in evangelism and he told me it was simply in obedience to the Great Commission (Matt 28) and not because his evangelism accomplished anything. This might seem like the wayward application of a maturing Christian who hasn't quite thought things through but it is more common than that.

In fact, we have already cited another example in this paper. When contemplating whether or not baptism does *anything*, this theologian said that the 'spiritual benefit' to believers is "the blessing of God's favor *that comes with obedience*, as well as the joy that comes through public professions of one's faith, and the reassurance of having a clear physical picture of dying and rising with Christ and of washing away sins."

We do not baptize, then, because it does anything but simply because it is commanded. The natural inclination to be consistent kicks in, so that we end up seeing the same sort of reasoning brought to bear on evangelism, the Lord's Supper, apologetics, and even education. These and other things we were commanded to do, but on account of notions about God's sovereignty, we are led to believe that we do them only for our own personal edification. (This is absurd in its own way, since obviously on this view even the obedience you perform was predestined, and there is no merit to your obedience since God determined that you would do it anyway.)

I do not wish to undermine the difficulty in trying to fathom the relationship between 'free will' and an omnipotent and omniscient God combined with our fallen and fallible nature. The Bible does say that those who believe are predestined and it does say that God has mercy on whom he has mercy and hardens those he hardens. It is abundantly clear, however, that God has, from the very beginning, deliberately chosen to use people as the very instrument by which he accomplishes certain things.

For example, Jonah surely would have received 'spiritual benefit' if he had immediately obeyed when called by God to go and preach to the Ninevites, and he was certainly chastened for his disobedience. Nonetheless, *if Jonah had not gone, Nineveh would have been ruined*. Or, if this be disputed, we can at least wonder why God would have sent a mere, pathetic mortal when he could have appeared in power before the people of Nineveh and issued the warning of judgment personally.

For some reason, God uses people. Who are we to challenge his choice, or dismiss it as an illusion? Example after example of this can be brought forward from both the Old and New Testaments of the Bible.

God used Esther to save his people, and this was accomplished by allowing the Jews to arm themselves, not because God split the earth open to swallow the enemies of Israel. God didn't *have* to send manna—he could have just made it so that the people weren't hungry. God used the prophet Nathan to accuse David even though God surely could have inflamed David's guilty conscience to agonizing proportions without the 'intermediary.' In the New Testament, when Jesus sent out the disciples and the 72 he need not have done so; he could have simply bent space and time to make it physically possible for He himself, perhaps through a multitude of Jesus-clones, to go out into the world preaching the arrival of the Kingdom of God. For that matter, He need not have sent the disciples to all nations baptizing; He could have gone Himself.

He certainly did not need anyone to circumcise eight day old males. He certainly didn't need to rely on circumcision (an act done by human hands) through which to join Jewish babies into the nation of Israel, and thereby be covered by the pledges and promises associated with this joining. He could have just declared it! He didn't need people to be involved at any point; no, but he chose to use them. Why should *this* pattern be broken under the new covenant?

Probably, much of the confusion here stems from the failure to understand that though the circumcision was an 'act done by human hands,' the joining of the young Jewish child into the nation of Israel was nonetheless *done by God*. It may be strange and mysterious that God would act in accordance to his promises when people perform certain actions, but the Scriptural witness is that, nonetheless, *He does so act.*

If there were doubt about this, the Donatists would be right.[19]

What if the difference between the old covenant practice of circumcision and the new covenant practice of baptism is not the involvement of people, but the fact that God does not constrain himself to baptism as a means of uniting people with Christ's body (as opposed to Israel's 'body' as in circumcision) but does so *too* through the faith produced by those who hear and receive the Gospel of Christ?

No good intentions or good will was sufficient to have God bind a person to the 'body' of Israel. One must be circumcised; period, end of story. But not so with the new covenant, for even though we are taking a very high view of baptism on this telling, and could even say that it is necessary, it is evident that we cannot say it is absolutely required. As it is written in Mark 16:16: "Whoever believes and is baptized will be saved, but whoever does not believe will be condemned." (I am aware that this portion of Mark isn't as well attested as the rest of the New Testament.) This passage clearly marks baptism as important but issues the declaration of condemnation based on absence of belief.

It may be said that if it is belief that counts—as is surely the case—why have baptism at all? Might we not say that a person who believes need not get baptized, and if he does so find ourselves returning simply to the merits of 'the spiritual benefits of obedience'?

There certainly are spiritual benefits of obedience but that doesn't mean that baptism accomplishes nothing, even when a person has seemingly already obtained that which is promised in baptism. But I am getting ahead of myself.

All this talk about using people can be summarized under the umbrella concept that "God uses means." That is, he

---

[19] Or, if baptism does nothing, it was a historic argument about nothing.

could do all sorts of things by simple declaration and arbitrary and capricious action which he initiates and carries out all on his own, *but he doesn't*. It seems bizarre that God would allow someone to suffer everlasting punishment because missionaries didn't get there in time, that's just the way it is. The book of Romans makes even this bizarre thing all the more bizarre by assuring us that these same will actually deserve that punishment! (Romans 1:20)

God uses means. He uses the 'stuff' of this world to carry out his divine purpose. The central and defining example of this is the Incarnation itself: Immanuel, God with us, God made Flesh.

In stark contrast to Gnosticism which would have us believe that all the important things are the hidden and secret 'spiritual' things, and that flesh and the created physical universe are nasty and evil coverings, Christianity says that when God created the universe (and man) he said that they were *good*. God became flesh, and in doing so illustrated again that he uses means from within our universe of experience in order to achieve his divine will. If God is capricious, it is in this—for an unknown reason, *he uses means.*[20]

However, I find that no more baffling than that he would have created us in the first place.

The many passages that talk about our sinful flesh need to be balanced against this pervasive pattern of using 'stuff.' This pattern was not abandoned in the new covenant. It was, as already explained, embraced, expanded, transfigured, transposed, and glorified.

It will be said, "But Colossians 2 clearly says, 'In him also you were circumcised with a circumcision made without hands, by putting off the body of the flesh, *by the circumcision of Christ*...' So Christ is the agent performing the circumcision." But read on to the very next word: "...

---

[20] Actually, I think I have some clue as to his reasons. By using people he grants us dignity and purpose. He must honor our mistakes as well as our victories in order for these to have genuine meaning.

having been buried with him in baptism, in which you were also raised with him through faith in the powerful working of God, who raised him from the dead."

This circumcision is indeed done by Christ, but it is unequivocally associated with baptism.

There is hostility towards the idea that Lutherans (and Catholics) believe they are 'saving' people or 'creating faith' in baptism, but this is really, truly, missing the mark.[21] We are told over and over again that in this event, performed by men, it is God who does the work, and this by burying us with Jesus in his death and then raising us with Jesus in his resurrection.

Other passages are explicit about precisely *how* the salvation happens.

For example, 1 Peter 3:18-22, and in particular 20-21, is explicit:

> ... in [the ark] a few, that is, eight persons, were

---

[21] To be frank, I don't particularly like the 'creating faith' phraseology, but not because of its alleged usurping of God's action. Rather than say, 'creating faith,' I think something like 'putting someone into a relationship with Jesus' would be better because it is technically more accurate, although this would require elaboration on what I think the Bible means by 'faith.' Conventionally, we think of 'faith' as simply one's personal, abstract 'belief.' I think this fuels some of the animosity towards a Lutheran view of baptism. I believe that the word has relational connotations that are easier seen today in the concept of 'trust.' Even that doesn't do it justice; Scripturally, it has *organic* connotations.

What really happens through faith is that one is brought into a relationship with Christ, much as we would say that someone who is adopted into a family has a relationship with the parents and his fellow siblings. Adopting people as infants is a normal human occurrence. It is odd that God should be unable to do *at least* as much. But this relationship is even more organic than this analogy suggests. We are *in* Christ. That is what it means to be saved. Some object to the idea that baptism could cause 'regeneration.' It is unfathomable, however, that one could actually be *in Christ* and yet remain unchanged, or change for the worse. Whatever ambiguity we may think there is regarding baptism, the Scripture is clear that baptism is directly connected to being 'buried with Christ.'

brought safely through water. Baptism, which corresponds to this, *now saves you*, not as a removal of dirt from the body but as an appeal to God[22] for a good conscience, *through the resurrection of Jesus Christ...*

The hasty reader sometimes concludes that the symbol here is 'baptism,' but a closer read reveals that it is the Flood and the Ark that is the symbol, and the thing they are symbolizing is baptism. It is also interesting to see that this baptism doesn't happen by the 'removal of dirt;' so often readers of a certain theological persuasion are quick to focus on the 'washing' aspect of baptism. This is a mistake. In baptism, the cleansing properties of water are secondary to the killing properties of water.

So how does the Flood and the Ark symbolize baptism? Well, the Flood waters obviously correlate to the waters of baptism; let us recall that the Flood involved the literal death of the planet, apart from eight who were spared by being 'in' an ark. In baptism, we too are put to death, but by our inclusion in the actual body of Christ, by being 'in Christ,' we are saved. How again? The passage tells us: "It saves you ... *through* the resurrection of Jesus Christ."

Note that the symbol itself was a real event involving real water, a real death, a real ark, and a real saving. Some maintain that this series of realities symbolizes a symbol of a metaphoric death, an analogous ark, and an allegorical saving. This is another example of construing the old covenant as having more reality than that which is in the new

---

[22] On the face of things, the idea of 'an appeal to God for a good conscience ' would seem to suggest a 'believer's baptism' understanding here but I believe the phrase really amounts to the doctrine of justification in different words. Rather than argue that here, I think the weight of the argument I've already laid out for this reading of Peter is already strong enough that even if we found warrant for a personal declaration of faith as being a component in baptism, this would not override my argument.

covenant. That is in flat contradiction to the pattern of the Scriptures.

Peter's logic, however, is clear: just as the real ark really saved people, so too does being united with the Christ-Ark really save, and this happens *through* baptism, by the *resurrection* of Jesus Christ.

No Lutheran is under any illusions about Who is actually performing the mighty deed. If God deems to use a person, by proclamation of word or by administration of water or whatever else, then that is up to God.

Lurking beneath all of this is the real point of friction: infant baptism. Probably, someone of a Reformed mindset could tolerate much of the understanding described above, because at least insofar as baptizing adults goes, Lutheran baptism 'looks' the same as their baptism. They would likely disagree with the understanding, but since practice wasn't affected, they'd let it slide. However, since Lutherans baptize infants, that poses a real problem.

It is often said by them that the practice is wholly unbiblical. They will especially cite the fact that there aren't any passages that explicitly allow for the baptizing of infants. Personally, if it is agreed that baptism correlates to circumcision, which Colossians 2 absolutely shows, and it is agreed that male children were circumcised at the age of eight days old, I would contend that no further Scriptural demonstration is required to justify this practice. If you know the details about old covenant circumcision and know that baptism is the new covenant replacement, the inference that just as male infants were circumcised so too (at least) can male infants be baptized. At the very least, one has to dispense with the notion that it is 'wholly unbiblical.'

Then, taking into account what we've said about the exponential potency of the new covenant in relation to their old covenant counterparts, we would quickly infer that baptism would include females, as well. If this pattern is not clear enough, consult Galatians 3:27-28 which says plainly, "For as many of you as **were baptized** into Christ have put on Christ. There is neither Jew nor Greek, there is neither slave nor free, there is no male and female, for you are all one in Christ Jesus."

I would have the reader note that once again, there is the explicit connection between this 'oneness in Christ' which is not limited by race, gender, or nationality, and being baptized into Christ. There is much talk about Galatians 3:28. Always forgotten is Galatians 3:27.

On this reading of the Scriptures, asking "should infants be baptized" is only a meaningful question at all if you believe 'baptism' refers only to a public declaration and commitment associated with a symbolic cleansing by water. If that is the case, one will naturally chafe at the notion that an infant could be baptized, for obviously an infant is unable to make public declarations and would derive no sustenance from remembering his or her ceremonial dip.

But it is precisely this view that is undermined by a Lutheran understanding of baptism. If one conceives of 'baptism' as a means by which God joins a person in the very body of Christ so that he is present in both the death and the resurrection of Jesus, one never wonders if the promise applies to infants, or if it is age-limited. Why would you? Baptism is about God's action, not man's. One is only appealing to a promise that God has made. We may think of Peter's words, in Acts 2, "For the promise is for *you and for your children* and for all who are far off, everyone whom the Lord our God calls to himself." Which promise?[23]

---

[23] The numerous passages in the book of Acts are less helpful in hashing out doctrine systematically then commonly realized because Acts *describes* the first generation of Christians and the early rise of the Church. What is *described* is not always what is *prescribed*. Moreover, the passages in the book of Acts do not say what baptism is or what it does so much as it says that they did, in fact, baptize. I am not denying that nuggets of insight cannot be extracted from the book of Acts on baptism, I am just pointing out that the proper way to develop an understanding of a doctrine is to begin with the clearer, more explicit passages that expressly aim to teach, and these are not in the book of

The one referenced immediately beforehand, of course, where Peter says that one will receive the gift of the Holy Spirit.

Thus, from a "Lutheran" perspective on baptism, the age of the person being baptized is irrelevant. None of the passages cited to this point specify an age limit, and if anything imply that God is prepared to honor his promises regarding baptism regardless of age. See in particular the Colossians passage which refers specifically to circumcision, which would have been understood by the readers to be a normal occurrence for male infants, but certainly not limited to them, since even grown foreigners who wished to become Jewish had to comply with it, or the Acts 2 passage just cited, where Peter says explicitly that the promise applies to children, along with everyone else.

PART THREE

What has been written so far may provide some insight into a Lutheran way of looking at baptism, but it still may not console some Christians who see baptism as a mere ritual or ceremony. They feel compelled to view it this way because it is clear enough from other Scriptures that ritual and ceremony cannot and does not save. And yet, Jesus did institute it, so there must be a reason! However, to them, suggesting that baptism might *do something* is tantamount to re-introducing legalism, the very thing that they see Jesus as liberating humanity from. They may even point to other passages in Colossians to support this view.

It should surely be a real head-scratcher, then, when 'conservative' Lutherans forcefully denounce legalism or works-righteousness or staunchly uphold the claim that only God can save. Having known more than a few Lutherans, I can attest to their abiding hatred for legalism. Does not their perspective on baptism fly in the face of all of this? Anyone

---

Acts.

who has read the writings of Martin Luther will be left with no doubt that he abhorred works-righteousness of all kinds! He was not known to be ambiguous. Yet he was also a staunch proponent of a view of baptism that is approximately what has been described above.

How is this to be reconciled?

Either Lutherans are maddeningly confused individuals, or else they see something else happening in baptism, which they too believe is supported in the Scriptures. In the first two parts of this essay, I have endeavored to give insight as to what they see is happening. But there is yet another side of this: the furious passion that Lutherans themselves are known to have in reaction to the so-called "believer's baptism."

On the "believer's baptism" view, the Gospel itself is insulted if anyone insinuates that God's grace could be mediated through the means of water or wine or bread. On the Lutheran view, the Gospel is not just insulted, *it is decimated*, by a "believer's baptism" perspective, because it strikes out at the Incarnation itself and the promise of salvation, as outlined in the Scriptures. Surely, readers can hazard some guesses as to why that might be from the foregoing. Clearly, there is much at stake no matter which view you take, but to understand the depths of concern a Lutheran might have, we need to spend a little bit more time expanding on themes we've already covered.

One of the problems with the "believer's baptism" perspective is that if it was logically extended, it is indistinguishable from a gnostic point of view in regards to the central character in Christianity, Jesus, the Christ.[24] That is to say, the objections to the Lutheran views on the sacraments, if valid, equally apply to Jesus himself. We also tend to see in these objections an emphasis on the 'spiritual' over and against the 'physical.'

---

[24] I do not say they *are* gnostic. I say only that one would be hard-pressed to tell them apart in some important respects.

What are the concerns raised against a sacramentalist view of baptism? That it is a ceremony or rite, that it is 'done by the hands of men', that it seems to save, even though elsewhere it is said that we are saved by grace alone. (One of Martin Luther's favorite passages, by the by!)

I responded to this by pointing out that God has already made it plain that he intends to bring salvation to the world through the work of his Church—that is, through the efforts of men and women. But it goes further: if we really wish to minimize the role of these men and women on the grounds often raised against Lutheran baptism, the arguments ought to also apply to Jesus himself.

Was not Jesus a real man?

When he rose from the dead, was it as a ghost, or was it as a transformed, yet fully real and substantial *man*?

The logic underlying these objections have the potential to eat through everything in Christianity.

Consider an analogy.

It is often said that technology is neutral. A gun, for example, can be put to good uses or bad uses. A counter-argument, though, is that no technology is neutral. For example, the presence of a gun in, say, a classroom, changes the dynamic within the room, regardless of whether or not the one with the gun is a very bad man or a police officer. It may be hard to measure the impact, but it can't be said that the gun's impact is neutral. It does have an effect.

But if one were to extend this logic to its logical end, then one would have to conclude that everything in existence can properly be regarded as 'technology.' What is a gun, after all, except a particular combination of atoms and electrons which can be put to various uses? Surely the same could be said about a human hand? Shall we now think of a human hand as a piece of technology? Some would. What about a rock that one happens to find in a field? There it sits—until someone decides to pick it up, perhaps to bash someone's head in with it or use as a foundation for a house. What about the ocean? One could drown their friend in it, or use it as a means of transportation. Should we consider the ocean a bit of technology? If so, should we therefore say that it, too, is not 'neutral'?

Before you know it, we've rendered the very term 'technology' as useless. It doesn't describe anything in particular. One may equally use the word 'universe.'

And yet, it must be admitted that none of these things are neutral. They certainly have an impact and change the dynamics of a situation! We can escape (to some degree) the logical progression into incoherency by defining 'technology' in such a way that it doesn't encompass everything in existence and with the clarification that technology is *morally* neutral.

The point of this analogy is to illustrate that if we are not careful, our argument can be extended to include many more things than we would like to see included.

So, take for example the argument against the Lutheran view of baptism that says that it cannot possibly hold water because, well, it gives magical powers to water. How could water do such things as Lutherans suggest it does in baptism? Flesh gives birth to flesh, but spirit gives birth to spirit, right?[25]

Isn't a person mostly water? Wasn't Jesus a person?

Does Jesus not save, since, as a person, he was mostly water?

Or it might be said that "faith comes from hearing the word."

Who hears the word? People—consisting of mostly water. How is the word received? By vibrations of the ear drum caused by vibrations of the air caused by the mouth and vocal cords of a person—who consists mostly of water. The exhale that causes those vibrations? In large part, moisture.

Does the word not save, since the word is transmitted by water, through water, to water?

---

[25] One will still hear this objection even after making pains to explain that it is not at all the case that it is the water by itself that is doing anything.

The gnostics held that matter is bad and the spiritual is good. Arguing that God could not, or would not, work through matter in regards to baptism and the Lord's Supper, implies that there is something intrinsically inferior about matter, and yet the whole mystery of the Gospel is that the Good took on Matter for our sake.

Did not the Spirit hover over the waters, before the fall of man? Did not God create everything and then declare that it was "good!" While we are at it, are not demons spiritual creatures? I guess the 'spiritual' is not automatically 'good' after all!

Clearly, if we wish to ensure that our objections do not spread backwards so that they do not undermine Jesus' own ability to save (and few Christians want to do that!) or lapse into what sounds the same as a gnostic repudiation of that which God called Good, we'll have to stop the logical progression by introducing distinctions and clarifications.

More to the point, the whole heart of the Gospel centers on this notion that God entered the world—really—as a person—really, in order to save a fallen people. To do so, he had to incarnate, that is, take on flesh. He ate, he drank, he laughed, he urinated, he slept. He was mostly water, just like us! When he spoke the very words of God, they came out of a mouth which vibrated atoms and molecules in the air which then vibrated the ear bones of his listeners where it was transmitted to their brains—mostly water—for interpretation. Jesus did not communicate telepathically (excuse me, 'spiritually') with his fellow Jews! God entered creation as part of his creation and interacted with humanity through his creation.

It is precisely because of this that he was able to save creation.

Is this not the logic as displayed in Hebrews 2?

> Since therefore the children share in flesh and blood, he himself likewise partook of the same things, that through death he might destroy the one

who has the power of death, that is, the devil, and deliver all those who through fear of death were subject to lifelong slavery. For surely it is not angels that he helps, but he helps the offspring of Abraham. Therefore he *had to* be made like his brothers in every respect, *so that* he might become a merciful and faithful high priest in the service of God, to make propitiation for the sins of the people. For *because* he himself has suffered when tempted, *he is able* to help those who are being tempted. [Italics added.]

We have now returned to the book of Hebrews, with all of its talk about shadows, images, and heavenly realities.

To say that God cannot use water (and wine and bread) to implement his plan of salvation is to say that God cannot use people to save people, which is to say that Jesus cannot save people, which is to say something utterly obscene, from a Christian point of view.

It may be hard to fathom how God might use his creation in order to mediate our salvation, but it does not seem to change the fact that he did, in the person of Christ. Why he should *have* to cease doing so in baptism is equally unfathomable. Sure, if there weren't Scriptures that suggested he did so, we wouldn't needlessly invoke it. But there *are* Scriptures where a plain reading seems to require that he *does something* in baptism. Who are we to object?

I would submit to the reader that God's use of water in this way is not arbitrary.

At the beginning, there was the waters of creation. Then, there was killing of the earth in the waters of the flood.[26] Each new human is born in the waters of their mother's womb. When Jesus' heart was stabbed on the cross, water gushed out. Why should it be the case that God would not,

---

[26] See 2 Peter 3:5-6 where Peter takes 'scoffers' to task for forgetting that in the beginning God made everything by water and then through the same means destroyed life on the earth. 'Water' is evidently a very serious thing.

when it suits him, bring new, spiritual life, through water?

Before Jesus said that 'flesh comes from flesh and spirit comes from spirit,' he did tell Nicodemus, "Truly, truly, I say to you, *unless one is born of water* and the Spirit, he cannot enter the kingdom of God." Maybe he wasn't joking. The passage does not say, "unless one is born of the Spirit."

No one disputes that God could have made it so that we are born again only by the Spirit alone, but it does not seem that this is the way he chose to act. Maybe there is something much more profound about reality than we suppose, and Christian baptism is meant, in part, to give us a glimpse into such things.

PART FOUR:
Arguments from Incredulity

I have alluded to various objections to Lutheran baptism. In my experience, even when the objections are put forward in theological terms, the real issue is often this: *the person just can't believe it.* The whole paradigm seems incredible to them. It's almost as if the theological objections emerge after the fact to justify their incredulity.

They are in good company. Those who first heard Jesus speak were also incredulous. What is interesting, to me, is that Jesus didn't try to show how what he was saying made perfect sense. People either accepted what he said... or they did not. When they didn't, he didn't chase them down to correct their 'misunderstandings.'

These people, of course, were Jews. They believed in God. Nonetheless, they held firm beliefs about what God wouldn't do and what he couldn't do.

The Gospel of John provides several examples of this, and I would submit that they are all related. They all involve people who believed in God arguing with God about what God might do. They all speak to how *they think* God will interact with his creation. In each case, Jesus says something that utterly flummoxes them, and then when they protest, he doubles-down on what he said. My belief is that the Jews were struggling mighty to understand the full mystery of the Incarnation, and coming up short.

Take John 3, where the theologian Nicodemus delicately wonders how it is that God could be with Jesus—as he clearly was. Jesus tells Nicodemus: "Truly, truly, I say to you, unless one is born again he cannot see the kingdom of God." Nicodemus is rightly confused: "How can a man be born when he is old? Can he enter a second time into his mother's womb and be born?" He is incredulous.

Jesus does not make things any clearer. He adds fuel to the confusion: "Truly, truly, I say to you, unless one is born **of water** and the Spirit, he cannot enter the kingdom of God."

This is a passage that causes considerable consternation for advocates of the "believer's baptism" perspective. All would be well, except for the inclusion of the word 'water' here. But imagine poor Nicodemus![27]

It would be fun to get into some contemporary alternative explanations for this, such as the view that 'born of water'

---

[27] John also doesn't explicitly refer to the institution of "The Lord's Supper", but his retelling of Jesus' insistence that his flesh is 'real' food and his 'blood' is real drink in chapter 6 more than compensates for this 'omission.' Jesus definitely instituted both the Lord's Supper and baptism, yet neither are referenced *as institutions* in the Gospel of John. Perhaps it isn't that they aren't referenced, but that there is something deeper afoot! In John 6 people also left the scene, incredulous. And Jesus let them go. He did not correct them—an odd thing to do, if in fact they had misunderstood him!

It is perhaps significant that it is also in John where Jesus turns water into wine, his first miracle. Few Christians doubt that Jesus did this or believe that he could not do this. But if he can turn water into wine, what is so hard to believe that through his declaration, wine could really be his blood? Jesus told the Jews that his flesh was real food, after he had fed 5,000 of them with a few loaves of bread. If he can turn a few loaves into hundreds, by his declaration, what is so hard to believe about the idea that by his same powerful word, we could receive his very body in the bread of the Lord's Supper? Are the objections to this theological? Or are they from incredulity? *Don't we know Who it is we're talking about?*

refers just to our 'physical' birth. On this view, in other words, unless you exist (ie, were born the first time) you cannot be born again. You could prepend anything with that caveat: "How do I get my driver's license?" Answer: "You must exist. Then you must stand in line for three hours at the DMV." At which point you will wish you didn't exist. Jesus may just as well say, "Unless you exist, you cannot be saved." I don't think anyone would think this is a very great insight by Jesus, here. I don't wish to dwell on this interpretation so much as to submit that the real problem is that even though Jesus explicitly uses the word 'water,' people just can't bring themselves to believe God would really use water in bringing about 'new births.'

Nicodemus persists: "*How* can these things be?" Jesus throws up his hands:

> Are you the teacher of Israel and yet you do not understand these things? Truly, truly, I say to you, we speak of what we know, and bear witness to what we have seen, but you do not receive our testimony. If I have told you earthly things and you do not believe, how can you believe if I tell you heavenly things?

This, I take to mean, "You believe in God and are seeing these things with your own eyes and you still have trouble believing it? *Really?*"

Not only is he amazed at Nicodemus's incredulity, but he is under the impression that Nicodemus should be perfectly primed, based on his knowledge, to understand 'heavenly' things. See the book of Hebrews.

It is a slight tangent, but since it seems to me that so much resistance to the Lutheran idea of baptism is created by the idea that infants can be baptized, this passage may have some bearing. It is often said that a baptism can have no value to an infant, because the infant will have no recollection of it. That, again, presumes the value of baptism is in its devotional appeal, and does *nothing*, which is the very thing being debated. But not one of us, I dare say, had any say in their physical birth! I know that I wasn't consulted prior to my conception! Who recalls their trip down the birth canal? Nobody.

Even on the idea that being 'born again' does not refer at all to baptism, it surely suggests that we are within our rights to entertain the idea that just as we do not recall the details of our physical birth, and just as we had no 'say' in it, so too do we have no 'say' in our spiritual birth, and it is not at all necessary that we remember the details of that, either.

Thus, if God can give someone New Life without them being aware of it at the time, though they be older, it is not out of line to think he could do the same, even if they are quite young. Even if they are an infant.

In any case, the whole idea of being 'born again' strongly suggests that the focus of our consideration is not supposed to be on our individual experience of our spiritual awakening, but on God's actions and promises concerning it. The emphasis is not trivial. Many attempts to avoid legalism end up in more legalism because of the trend to link our salvation to our own efforts to be holy: as if *that* is what it means to be a spiritual being.

No. Like begets like. Flesh can only give birth to flesh. To be a spiritual being you must be born from a spiritual being. You cannot possibly 'holy' yourself into it. Please remember that the Bible does not think of 'spiritual' and 'heavenly' as 'ghostly' leftovers of our life on the earth, but quite the opposite. See 1 Corinthians 15; and remember that Jesus, when he rose from the dead, ate with his disciples, to dispel their fear that he was a ghost. The tendency to equate 'spiritual' with 'ghostly' is not new to our age.

The next instance of incredulity in the Gospel of John is found in chapter 6. The people ask Jesus: "What must we do, to be doing the works of God?"

Jesus says, "This is the work of God, that you believe in him whom he has sent."

This is apparently too easy an answer, so the Jews then

demand a sign. Moses, at least, was able to send down bread from heaven, they say. Jesus shakes his head at this; he knows something about heavenly bread, that is, 'realer' bread. Since they are not satisfied with the easy answer, he gives them the rock bottom truth: 'Unless you eat *me,* you will die.' This is too much:

> The Jews then disputed among themselves, saying, "How can this man give us his flesh to eat?" So Jesus said to them, "Truly, truly, I say to you, unless you eat the flesh of the Son of Man and drink his blood, you have no life in you. Whoever feeds on my flesh and drinks my blood has eternal life, and I will raise him up on the last day. For my flesh is true food, and my blood is true drink. Whoever feeds on my flesh and drinks my blood abides in me, and I in him. As the living Father sent me, and I live because of the Father, so whoever feeds on me, he also will live because of me. This is the bread that came down from heaven, not like the bread the fathers ate, and died. Whoever feeds on this bread will live forever."

Even his own disciples now say, "This is a hard saying; who can listen to it?" Jesus then does with them what he did with Nicodemus: 'You see all the things I'm doing and you still don't believe? Why, I guess I'll just rise from the dead, then! We'll see if that helps!' John then reports: "After this many of his disciples turned back and no longer walked with him."

There is no record in John that Jesus chased after them to 'clarify' his position.

It is interesting, and I would even say powerfully revealing, that John does not specifically mention either the institution of baptism or the Lord's Supper in his book. He was writing last of all the Gospel authors, when these institutions would have been well established and known to the church, but he does not state them by name. John 3 and

John 6, in my opinion, provide a radical perspective on these institutions—if one can get past their incredulity.

After all, we do believe in a God who came to the planet and died and rose for our sake, no?

I would submit that in the sacramentalist approach to these institutions, we have on display the great mystery of the incarnation. We shouldn't find it so hard to believe since we have the evidence of the resurrection. The poor Jews did not have this witness, and had to wrestle with Jesus' claims to be God based on lesser demonstrations.

Once again, John records the exchange, this time in chapter 10: "How long will you keep us in suspense? If you are the Christ, tell us plainly."

Jesus answers them directly, "I told you, and you do not believe."

In other words, the problem is not that he didn't tell them, but that they won't accept what he is telling them. Once again, Jesus doubles-down: "I and the Father are one."

Modern readers don't understand the import of this, but the Jews did. It went down like this:

> The Jews picked up stones again to stone him. Jesus answered them, "I have shown you many good works from the Father; for which of them are you going to stone me?" The Jews answered him, "It is not for a good work that we are going to stone you but for blasphemy, because you, being a man, make yourself God."

Jesus submitted his own works to them, which everyone knew could only be done by God (remember Nicodemus's opening lines to Jesus, earlier), but this was not enough. They say that the problem is that he is claiming to be God, and this certainly is the theological manifestation of the issue. The wrap their disbelief in the cloak of 'protecting God's sovereignty' or 'holiness' or whatever, but I think the real problem *is they just can't believe it.* The theological objection is a mask for their 'gut' reaction.

Jesus is not above throwing bombs. He's already informed the Pharisees that if they want to enter the Kingdom of God they'll have to become spiritual infants undergoing a real birth (through water and the Spirit). He's told them all that unless people eat his flesh and drink his blood, they have no life in them. Now, to Jews, who were as fierce in their monotheistic allegiance as the Muslims are today, he says, basically, "What's the problem believing that I could be God? Doesn't the scriptures that you accept already say that everybody is a god?"

> Jesus answered them, "Is it not written in your Law, 'I said, you are gods'? If he called them gods to whom the word of God came—and Scripture cannot be broken—do you say of him whom the Father consecrated and sent into the world, 'You are blaspheming,' because I said, 'I am the Son of God'? If I am not doing the works of my Father, then do not believe me; but if I do them, even though you do not believe me, believe the works, that you may know and understand that the Father is in me and I am in the Father."

Unmoved, they sought to arrest him. There is no record that Jesus sought to clarify his position, or remove the impression that he left that every person was God incarnate. He just left.

Just a few chapters later, Jesus would cement his claim to be God himself, incarnate on the land, by doing what no person could conceivably do: raise Lazarus from the dead.

They still couldn't believe it. It was immediately after this that they decided that Jesus must die.

Given this pattern in the Gospel of John, it probably shouldn't surprise anyone that it was John who records the account of 'Doubting Thomas.' Or, even after being seen several times, and eating with them, which no ghastly creature would do, when Jesus invited them to breakfast, "none of the disciples dared to ask him, 'Who are you?' They knew it was the Lord." They knew it, but they just couldn't get past their incredulity.

In the context of responding to incredulity, I wish to call attention again to Colossians 2:9.

Here it is:

> For in [Christ] the whole fullness of deity dwells bodily, and you have been filled in him, who is the head of all rule and authority. In him also you were circumcised with a circumcision made without hands, by putting off the body of the flesh, by the circumcision of Christ, having been buried with him in baptism, in which you were also raised with him through faith in the powerful working of God, who raised him from the dead.

In my reference to the Gospel of John, I tried to show how the argument from incredulity against the Lutheran view of baptism (and by extension, the Lord's Supper) not only extends to the Incarnation itself, but is answered by it. If you believe that God incarnated on the earth, and proved it by rising from the dead, the other stuff shouldn't be hard to believe, either. Moreover, if you disbelief the latter, you may as well disbelieve the former. But in this passage from Colossians, you see the progression plainly.

Earlier, we addressed the connection between circumcision and baptism part, but pay special attention now to the fact that Paul precedes all of that with a clear reference to the Incarnation. He directly states that God is present in his "whole fullness" in the person of Christ. This is the immediate context, and the basis that Paul draws upon when he explains what happens when we are "buried with [Christ] in baptism." Paul might say that if you doubt the reality of the latter, on the basis of incredulity, you may as well doubt the former.

I think he would be quite right to make that argument. All agree that orthodox Christianity holds that Jesus was not only God, but also truly man. But if we probe deeper, we realize that orthodox Christianity not only maintains the transcendent nature of God, *but also his immanent nature.* That is to say, on this view of who God is, there is no point in creation where God is not present in his fullness. If you believe *that*, to get hung up on him being uniquely present "bodily" is absurd. In Jesus, he is only doing something he was always doing, anyway! In Jesus, he was making it visibly known.

Is it so hard to imagine that an immanent God, who is always present in his fullness in every corner of creation, and was uniquely present 'bodily' in Christ, could not also be present in his "whole fullness" elsewhere or elsewise in *his* creation? Say... in water, bread, and wine?

I will be the first to concede that there can be well-meaning 'pure' theological attempts to understand baptism (and the Lord's Supper) that are not merely masks for incredulity. I have argued, on a theological basis, that these attempts fail for a number of reasons, and have a bearing on a number of other important theological points. But incredulity... that is a different animal altogether. We can understand incredulity within the atheistic community, but it shouldn't drive the views of those within the Christian community!

This incredulity threatens to unravel not just the role of baptism in our death and resurrection, but the very incarnation of God, and indeed, immanence itself; that is, our understanding of God as both a transcendental and immanent God is at stake. If you're not careful, you may end up dispensing with God completely, for all *practical* intents and purposes. After all, it isn't like he actually, really, interacts with reality, right? At least, I fear that we risk living as if this is so. We may ask ourselves, "If we live like that, are we quite sure we don't actually believe that?"

CONCLUSION

Through the course of my apologetics ministries, we often have conferences and conversations about the arts and literature. These are ecumenical gatherings, where I can say with all confidence each person desires the very heart of God. There may be slightly more Lutherans in the mix, but all denominations tend to be reflected. I often put forward a question along these lines:

"When we think of 'literary apologetics' we often think of those like C.S. Lewis, J.R.R. Tolkien, Flannery O'Conner, G.K. Chesterton, Graham Greene, and Dorothy Sayers. These seem to have a lasting influence with no sign that anyone like them will emerge today. Is it at all significant that they all also happen to be sacramentalists? They are all Anglicans or Catholics. Where are the Evangelicals?"

Every time this question has been posed, those with a "believer's baptism" point of view tend to wave off the possibility that the fact that all these authors believed in the real presence of God in the water, wine, and bread. The idea that the absence of similar authors today leaving their mark having to do with the fact that the Christian literary scene is dominated by those who reject such views is likewise waved off.

I do not think that is wise.

What a sacramentalist brings to the table is the firm conviction, lived out daily, that God *is present* in the dirt and grime of every day experience. He uses the weak, the frail, and the broken to glorify himself. The literature produced by these people resonate, I believe, because their stories reflect real life. Life is not lived in the ecstasy of the altar call. It is lived in the trenches and hand to hand combat with doubt, despair, and the temptations of the flesh.

To put it bluntly, I think that the non-sacramentalist views tend to create an expectation of a life filled with one 'spiritual' high after another, with daily (ecstatic) encounters with God. Reality dashes this expectation and can lead to disillusionment. However, to find out that God meets us *in all his fullness* in the gritty details and the mundane, suggests that there is hope for us yet.

If God can glorify himself through something as common as water, why, that's good news, because, after all, that's pretty much what we are. Water.

Why Do Christians Oppose Homosexuality When Even Jesus Didn't?

I am often asked to explain "what's so wrong" about homosexuality, from a Biblical point of view.

For example, many secularists believe that because Leviticus calls for the Jews to execute homosexuals, Christians ought to do the same, otherwise they are inconsistent—at least if they have a high view of the Christian Scriptures. Thus, they think that if I oppose homosexuality, I should also be advocating for their execution.[28]

It does tend to be the case that if one has a high view of the Christian Scriptures, a rejection of homosexuality tends to follow. Similarly, if one has a low view, there is great ambivalence on the question, if not outright acceptance of homosexuality. Fueling this 'low view' is the perception that it is in Old Testament where we see the most violent arguments against homosexuality. Jesus, on this view, was silent on the matter. Paul and John? Not silent, but they were mere men (read: culture-bound bigots), so what do they count for?

It is probably because Jesus is seen as being indifferent on homosexuality, and his biting attitude towards the rich and powerful, that prompts people of a certain ideological persuasion to give Jesus a pass. Moreover, the underlying assumption is that nothing can be regarded as essential to Christianity if its founder, Jesus the Christ, did not single it out for discussion. Thus, Jesus' silence on homosexuality is seen to speak volumes.

Jesus, in point of fact, was *not* silent on the matter. He was *emphatic*. People looking for proof texts will have

---

[28] There are so many things wrong with this view that basic theological education would dispense with, but this is not the time and place. Just to be clear, though: this may be a logical progression that secularists think is rational, but I emphatically do not.

trouble finding Jesus' remarks on the topic. In order to understand Jesus' positively *strident* views on the matter, one has to likewise dispense with scouring the Bible for proof texts. That's just not how the Bible was written or how it was intended to be read. Sure, in some areas we can find 'proof texts' on certain issues, and sometimes we get more direct affirmation or repudiation than in other cases, but it is not common that the writers themselves had that intent when they penned those passages.

The point is important. Most of the time, a writer was making an entirely different point, and we glean something else along the way. There is a danger in taking that point in isolation, paying no mind to the main point the author was making. This is the case both narrowly, within specific passages, chapters, and books, but it is also the case broadly, concerning the whole Bible. There is a main point to the Bible, and it is decidedly *not* to repudiate homosexuality. It is not even to establish a moral code.

The main point of the Bible is to make perfectly plain that mankind is in deep, deep trouble. According to the Scriptures, our only hope is to fall in with God's rescue plan. How much trouble are we in? Let's put it this way: according to the Bible, no matter how good you think you are, no matter how earnest your religious practice is, no matter how moral you are, not even if you are the World's Best Heterosexual™, such things *will not save you from the judgment to come.*

Trying to weasel out of different proscriptions and limits on our behavior is akin to the teachers of the law asking, "And just who is our neighbor?" The purpose of the question was really about justifying their behavior in the sight of God, so they started probing around the edges of what is allowed, tolerated, or excused. They wanted to find a way around the law while staying on God's good side.

What I am saying is important. This is not a theological observation. I am highlighting a timeless aspect of human nature.

Perhaps I can illustrate what I'm getting at by thinking about my life as a father. Anyone who has worked with kids will know what I mean. If I say, "I want you to clean your room before you use the computer," I can expect a barrage of questions like this: "But dear father, what if I think I might have cancer, and I need the computer for research? Surely that's more important than a clean room, right?" Or, "Father, I only want to use the computer to look at a map. I wasn't playing a game, *honest*..." Or what if I say, "You may have 2 cookies." One of them will surely say, "But can I have 3? I see that you didn't say I couldn't have three." You're right, kid. I said you could have 2, and 2 precludes 3. I don't need to preclude all the other options individually. I can affirm just one option, "Two cookies. Deal with it."

In other words, I can put out the thing that I want, but there are a million ways to try to get out of it. The *one thing* precludes the others. They needn't be mentioned specifically. The purpose of the line of questioning is to find a way to get what they want without being taken to task for being disobedient.

Homosexual behavior is just so; with it are any number of behaviors that are outside of God's stated desires. "But what if they love each other?" or "What if they are monogamous?" Or... "What if I want to have sex with a prostitute?" Or, "What if I want a divorce? You know, Moses let us get a divorce."

We could go on and on for hours and days imagining excuses for not doing what God says, just like every night my kids have a new reason for why they didn't brush their teeth when I told them to. A thousand variations of a thousand excuses are offered, but in the end, my request was the same: "Brush your teeth, and get ready for bed."

But the proof-texter would get out the family manual and say, "Well, see here. Once we were on a trip and we were in the car at night, and we didn't brush our teeth then..." And of course every parent knows what's going on. They're just trying to get out of doing something they don't want to do.

This phenomena explains in large part why you don't see long lists of precluded behaviors in the Scriptures. If God says, "Love!" but you can think of a thousand different reasons for why you *don't want to* and *won't*, God doesn't do us any favors by going into each objection and giving his argument against it. After all, the next person will have his own set of a thousand different reasons for why he won't love. Before you know it, the Bible is twenty million words long. Not long after that, it is fifty million, as each person invents new generalizations and rationalizations in a quest to escape the uncomfortable ramifications of a plainly stated command.

Homosexual behavior is justified and rationalized just like this. But just what *is it,* then, that God said? Where is Jesus plainly stated directives on homosexuality.

We need to start in the beginning, when God made man and woman.

> Then the man said, "This at last is bone of my bones and flesh of my flesh; she shall be called Woman, because she was taken out of Man." Therefore a man shall leave his father and his mother and hold fast to his wife, and they shall become one flesh. (Genesis 2:23-24 ESV)

I will make two important observations from this text. First of all, I note that the pattern–*before Man and Woman had even sinned*–is that marriage is something between a man and a woman.

Enter the Mormon of old, seeking to justify himself: "But it doesn't say ONLY one woman. And there are people in the Old Testament with more than one wives, and they are even people of faith..." Sure, and I can't think of a single instance where that worked out well... but for our purposes here, the important thing to note is that this person is just trying to wriggle out of what is otherwise pretty plain.

The second thing I observe in this passage is the assertion

that they will become *one flesh*.

Again, this all happens *before* sin has entered the world. In other words, this arrangement is established for humanity from the very beginning, right from the start, even in the Edenic paradise. We see that proscriptions and rules and requirements sometimes change in the Bible, for example when God comes to live with the Jews.[29] Do we have a good reason for believing this is one of them?

Genesis is at the beginning of the Old Testament. Let's skip to the end. Malachi 2:13-16 reads:

> And this second thing you do. You cover the LORD's altar with tears, with weeping and groaning because he no longer regards the offering or accepts it with favor from your hand. But you say, "Why does he not?" Because the LORD was witness between you and the wife of your youth, to whom you have been faithless, though she is your companion and your wife by covenant. Did he not make them one, with a portion of the Spirit in their union? And what was the one God seeking? Godly offspring. So guard yourselves in your spirit, and let none of you be faithless to the wife of your youth. "For the man who does not love his wife but divorces her, says the LORD, the God of Israel, says that he hates divorce...

Here we see a reference back to the Genesis formula: in marriage, a man and a woman have become one flesh. We find out the purpose of the one fleshness: because God wanted godly offspring. We learn that God takes this very seriously, declare in no uncertain terms that *he hates divorce*.

---

[29] The rules got harsher and more stringent, precisely because God came to live with them. When the President stays in your house, new rules apply. When he leaves, the rules are no longer necessary. God no longer lives with the Jews in a visible fashion. He is not visibly present anywhere, *now*, either.

The justifying attorneys chime in: "But what if the woman is old? Can I divorce her then? Oh wait, you answered that." Or, "What if she doesn't cook my favorite supper?" Or, "What if I see another woman that I'd rather be with?" The advocate for gay marriage adds, "I note that it doesn't specifically say that the man *can't be* married to one man or a woman to a woman."

The parent knows these are not sincere questions. The 'kid' just doesn't want to brush his teeth.

It should be observed that if God's plan for making them one flesh was so that there would be godly offspring, in the case of homosexuals, there are no offspring at all, godly or not. You know, by definition of the behavior. Over the last one hundred years, there has been massive push to separate sex from reproduction. We would be going too far to say that, Biblically, the sole purpose of sex is to have children, but passages like this one make it absolutely clear that *Christians* cannot adopt the modern attempt to divorce the two things. Having 'godly offspring' was a *pre-fall* purpose of sexuality, which we see explicitly reiterated at the closing of the old testament era.

"But they could adopt… or they could get a surrogate… they are just as loving and kind as heterosexuals…."

There has *got* to be some way you'll let me get into bed without brushing my teeth!

Now, the only person in the Bible who seems to hate divorce more than the Lord God of Israel is Jesus called the Christ.

> And Pharisees came up to him and tested him by asking, "Is it lawful to divorce one's wife for any cause?" He answered, "Have you not read that he who created them from the beginning made them male and female, and said, 'Therefore a man shall leave his father and his mother and hold fast to his wife, and the two shall become one flesh'? So they are no longer two but one flesh. What therefore God

has joined together, let not man separate."

They said to him, "Why then did Moses command one to give a certificate of divorce and to send her away?" He said to them, "Because of your hardness of heart Moses allowed you to divorce your wives, but from the beginning it was not so. And I say to you: whoever divorces his wife, except for sexual immorality, and marries another, commits adultery."

The disciples said to him, "If such is the case of a man with his wife, it is better not to marry." But he said to them, "Not everyone can receive this saying, but only those to whom it is given. For there are eunuchs who have been so from birth, and there are eunuchs who have been made eunuchs by men, and there are eunuchs who have made themselves eunuchs for the sake of the kingdom of heaven. Let the one who is able to receive this receive it." (Matthew 19:3-12 ESV)

Now primed to see it, we can spot the rationalizing and attempts to justify oneself carried out by the Pharisees and teachers of the law. "Isn't it lawful to get a divorce?" they ask, because of course they knew all about what God said in Malachi, but Moses said you *could* give the lady a certificate and dispose of her. Isn't it *legal*? they want to know—as if it were legal, that would excuse it.

Jesus puts the kabosh on this idea so emphatically, that even the disciples are like, "Holy crap. If we have to *actually stay* with the woman for the rest of our life, and it's adultery to leave her (except for sexual immorality), it might be better to not get married at all!"

But note Jesus' explicit citation of the Genesis formula: in the beginning, the Creator 'made them male and female.' For this reason, a man will leave his father and mother and be united to his wife, and the two will become *one flesh*. So they are no longer two, but one flesh.

We learn something new on Jesus' telling, although it was

already alluded to in Malachi: this one-fleshness is created *by the deliberate act of God*–"What therefore God has joined together, let not man separate."[30]

So, Jesus–and Christians believe Jesus is God, you may recall–goes all *the way back* to Genesis to state the original plan, and dispenses with all attempts to erect caveats or excuses. He specifically says it: "from the beginning it was not so" and specifically blames the 'exception' on their "hardness of heart." This is unequivocal.

The original plan was good when the world was perfect and unfallen, it was good while God lived with the Jews when they were a covenant nation, it was good after the covenant had been dissolved and the Jews were dispersed to the four winds, it was good when they were brought back together, and it was good when God again walked among men, but this time in the flesh. In a moment, we'll see that it was regarded as still good, even after Jesus died and rose from the dead, and disappeared from our sight. Conclusion: the plan is *still* good:

A man and a woman. One flesh. God does this. He has his reasons. You don't have to like it. He doesn't have to counter your every imagined relationship structure. This is the plan. One man, one woman, one flesh. God joins them. The *state* doesn't join them. God does it. They don't join themselves.

---

[30] It is worth noting that on my view, which assumes there is a God and that it is actually true that he made humanity just so, this 'one flesh' relationship is made by God in every case, whether people believe there is a God, or they don't. This essay has not been directed at the non-believer, *per se*, but if I'm right, what we observe in the real world (eg, according to 'natural law') will show that where this plan is implemented intact (realities of a fallen world, notwithstanding), there will be greater happiness, and where this plan is despised, pain and suffering will follow. Similarly, God made it so that our bones stay inside the flesh, and our arms are not made with the idea that they should be used as jack stands holding up automobiles. You can try an 'alternate' plan for your arm, and the compound fracture that follows should be expected. 'Alternate' plans for sexual relationships will also lead to 'compound fractures,' but of a relational sort. Sexually transmitted diseases... 'unwanted children'... etc.

God does it.

And now, dear rationalizer, you want to contemplate a divorce in light of how seriously God abhors it? By all means, go ahead, but don't kid yourself. It is outside of God's plan. *He does not approve.* Do you have any other sexual or relationship variations you'd like to propose? He's not going to counter them all with chapter and verse. He doesn't need to. He's said his piece. Now it is for you to obey... or not.

Now, as it happens, the Genesis passage gets cited in full once more in the New Testament and alluded to at least once more. Clearly, since God made all humans and established marriage before the fall, and then doubled down on it in Jesus, the Genesis pattern applies to all humans, everywhere, in any time or place, until the end of time. If Christianity is true, that is. But there are some extra considerations for Christians in particular, as the next citation shows. Ephesians 5:

> Husbands, love your wives, as Christ loved the church and gave himself up for her, that he might sanctify her, having cleansed her by the washing of water with the word, so that he might present the church to himself in splendor, without spot or wrinkle or any such thing, that she might be holy and without blemish. In the same way husbands should love their wives as their own bodies. He who loves his wife loves himself. For no one ever hated his own flesh, but nourishes and cherishes it, just as Christ does the church, because we are members of his body. "Therefore a man shall leave his father and mother and hold fast to his wife, and the two shall become one flesh." This mystery is profound, and I am saying that it refers to Christ and the church. However, let each one of you love his wife as himself, and let the wife see that she respects her husband. (Ephesians 5:25-33 ESV)

Note again the explicit quotation of Genesis 2. It's almost like all the people in the Bible believed that stuff! I thought Paul invented this bigotry! Honestly, I can't keep up with all the latest conspiracies. There is a twist, though: just as the man and the woman are one flesh, Christ and his Church are, too. Could this mean what it really sounds like it means? Is it really the case that just as in marriage *God* makes a man and a woman, literally, one flesh, through the power of the Spirit, *God* makes believers, literally, one flesh with Jesus? Why, if this were true, then it would mean that through sex, a believer might communicate his partner into the real body of Christ. Surely this cannot be so! Paul, could you clarify?

Paul, in 1 Corinthians 6:

> "All things are lawful for me," but not all things are helpful. "All things are lawful for me," but I will not be dominated by anything. "Food is meant for the stomach and the stomach for food"—and God will destroy both one and the other. The body is not meant for sexual immorality, but for the Lord, and the Lord for the body. And God raised the Lord and will also raise us up by his power. **Do you not know that your bodies are members of Christ? Shall I then take the members of Christ and make them members of a prostitute? Never! Or do you not know that he who is joined to a prostitute becomes one body with her? For, as it is written, "The two will become one flesh."** But he who is joined to the Lord becomes one spirit with him.[31] Flee from sexual

---

[31] Some (Christians) try to escape the plain implications of this passage by emphasizing the dichotomy between the flesh and the spirit. I cannot go into it here, but suffice it to say that the risen Lord's spiritual body was not unfleshly; Jesus proved to the disciples that he wasn't a phantasm by eating with them. See chapter fifteen in this same book by Paul for some discussion on bodies, fleshly and spiritual. Similarly, some (Christians) try to escape the ramifications of this passage, and downplay the implications regarding homosexuality, by insisting that all Paul is addressing here is monogamy. But Paul is quite clear, in his invocation of

immorality. Every other sin a person commits is outside the body, but the sexually immoral person sins against his own body. Or do you not know that your body is a temple of the Holy Spirit within you, whom you have from God? You are not your own, for you were bought with a price. So glorify God in your body. (1 Corinthians 6:12-20 ESV)

Why *yes*, it really does appear that by virtue of the fact that a man and woman have sex together, they have become one flesh–that is, God joins them in marriage–and by virtue of this man's relationship with Christ, he brings the woman with him into Christ. Or vice versa. Look just a few verses later, in 1 Corinthians 7:14, where Paul makes this explicit.

If you're not following the line of progression, pretend that someone puts water in his mouth and then gets in his car. Sure enough, the water is in the car, too. If A = B and B = C then A = C. One flesh, all the way around.

It would appear that in the Scriptures, old testament and new, this whole 'one flesh' thing is taken very seriously. Whether it is in the beginning or the end or the middle, whether it is the Law Giver of Moses or the Grace-bringer, Christ, God's plan for marriage, and what happens in marriage, remains. It is part of *the order of creation*. You may as well wish that gravity stopped working… "But God, I didn't *want* the person to go splat on the pavement when I pushed him off the building… I just thought it would be fun… How about an exemption? No? Then I'm going to pout."

---

the Genesis formula, how the prostitute is 'joined' with the one using her services. *It was through the sex*. This is indeed a difficult teaching. It is no wonder that so many would like to try to wriggle out of it. It certainly puts a new spin on the notion of 'pre-marital sex,' right? On this view, that phrase is a contradiction in terms: there is no such thing as 'pre-marital sex' because it is *through* sex that one is married, or joined together by God. Unless it can be shown that people availing themselves of a prostitute's services first obtained a license from the state or paid a fee…

This added insight provided to us by Paul about how the marital act is not only a pattern of Christ joined with all his believers but further, it is a real unity–just as the man and the woman having sex are made into a real unity–serves to drive home the point that *for Christians*, it is extremely, extremely important to abide by God's plan for marriage. Not because it saves us, mind you, but because in it we find out that evidently, God didn't establish the institution of marriage for arbitrary reasons. Here is a shocker: God, who made the universe and all that is in it, has good reasons for what he is doing, and these reasons are very likely in our best interest. Godly offspring, yes, but also, a pathway towards understanding the mystery of salvation: we are saved by virtue of the fact that we are in the literal body of Christ, and when that body stands up under the just punishment delivered by the Father, we are ourselves spared. (See Romans 6 and 1 Peter 3)

You can make excuses for why you don't like God's plan, and start looking for ways around it ("But I would have preferred *scientific* evidence..."), justifying–only to yourself–why you shouldn't be swept away in the flood of judgment. But it won't change the facts. God sent a lifeboat: it was Himself. All you had to do was climb in, but you preferred to inspect the hinges and kick the sides and hem and haw and dispute whether or not there was a need to be saved at all. "What I really wanted was a fancy yacht to pluck me out of these shark-infested waters! I'm not getting into *that*!" Now you're floating away to your doom. Whose fault is that? *C'est la vie.*

To bring this matter to a close, the Biblical case against homosexuality does not rest because God specifically addresses it, but because he emphatically affirms *something else*, and this something else precludes it. Likewise, we can imagine all sorts of variations of sexual behavior (any behavior, really) that are not emphatically and explicitly treated in the Bible. Does that mean all these ideas are on the table for consideration or pursuit? Not at all. The *something else* that God affirms precludes that other stuff.

I would like to note that I have not once cited any of the 'negative' passages often cited to defend the proposition that homosexuality is outside of God's plan. Not a word from Leviticus, you'll note. I think some of those passages are pretty clear-cut and decisive, but I also know how people pick and pick and pick at them, trying to get them to say (or be conceived as possibly saying) something that they do not say. I also know that the argument for God's plan for marriage explains why those passages would exist at all. And since God's plan for marriage is stated via positive affirmations, clearly and repeated constantly–in fact, affirmed by the Son of God–that seemed the better way to go.

At any rate, that is the main way I approach the question, and I think is very near to the answer, though of course much, much, much more could be said.

Homosexuality, especially in regards to 'gay marriage,' has become an incredibly charged political question. However, it does not follow automatically that what a Christian believes about marriage (or any other issue) is something that should be 'imposed' upon and within a society of non-believers. The converse is true: just because people have a certain view because they believe in God as revealed in the Christian Scriptures, it doesn't mean that they are not allowed to promote and defend that view in a society of non-believers... especially in a (theoretically) democratic society. This particular issue is worthy of further comment, but it is not the purpose of this essay.

Instead, I wish to draw the point that if I am right in the analysis I've laid out, this issue is non-negotiable for the Christian who has a high view of the Scriptures. The idea that marriage is a real union between one man and one woman is threaded throughout the entirety of Scriptures, and emphatically endorsed by the founder of the faith, Jesus the Christ; that is, by God. The real union created in a marriage between a man and a woman is put forth as a pattern for the real union that Jesus enjoys with his Church; that is, people. This idea that 'two can be one' is probably an object lesson for humanity trying to ponder the 'three in one' nature of a Triune God. There is more at stake, here, then how we utilize our genitalia.

There are, of course, Christians who see no problem with gay marriage or homosexuality. They too deserve further comment, but these same tend to have a low view of the Scriptures, so all of the above is likely to fall upon deaf ears. The reader was interested in why Christians tend to be opposed to homosexuality and gay marriage, and the ones that are tend to take a high view of the Scriptures, so that is the focus of this essay.

Yet it must be acknowledged that even people with very high views on the Scriptures will take issue with the points raised. I will only say that each of my points, and in many cases, the very logic itself, is grounded in the Scriptures themselves. For example, in my experience, the implications of the above on 'pre-marital sex' or the idea that through sex a believer could actually unite someone (say, a prostitute) with Christ, are very hard to swallow, but it is the Apostle Paul that makes that argument, not me. And he makes it in no uncertain terms.

Some try to avoid this 'problem' by marginalizing Paul, but as I have shown, Jesus was no less direct. We who have a high view of the Scriptures may be left with the uncomfortable task of simply having to obey what we read.

One of the great things about Jesus was the fact that he did not hesitate to speak in uncompromising terms about many issues. If he were only a great historic figure, we might take on ourselves the role of Arbiter in determining which things we'll take seriously and which we will not. However, this great historic figure—or so goes the story that I happen to believe is absolutely true—claimed to be God himself, the maker and author of the universe. Furthermore, he proved it by rising from the dead with powerful demonstrations that literally shook the history of mankind. I would submit that in the case of homosexuality we have just *one* instance of a whole series of examples where Jesus commanded difficult and unpleasant things, but we have no recourse except *to obey*. It is not a question of whether or not we like it, or understand it, or that we will through our obedience, be saved.

My strong suspicion, though, is that much that is strange and perplexing are things that will *only* become comprehensible through obedience. The Scriptures have some things to say about that, too. I'd start with what Jesus himself said about it, and go from there.

The reader is invited to consider the reasons why this piece by the famed children's author and sermon writer, George MacDonald, is included in this collection of essays.

Faith, the Proof of the Unseen

Preached in Brixton Congregational Church, Last Sunday Morning, June 1882. Originally published in *The Christian World Pulpit*, 1882.

By George MacDonald

Now faith is the substance of things hoped for, the evidence of things not seen.

—Hebrews 11:1

I read it to you as it is down here, but as it stands it never conveyed any idea to my mind at all, and I am very glad it is altered in the Revised Version, for, of all things if we are Christians—having the least claim to the name—it is with the spirit and not the letter that we have to do; and this translation has neither the letter nor spirit. Happy ought the man to be who finds the ark things in the dear Book cleared up for him—to find that what had been as a pebble under his feet was a nut with a kernel in it, a life in it, a power of growth planted within his spirit. The true heart goes to the blessed Book not as an idolater but as a disciple; not to worship the Book, but to learn the will of Him who made the Book, and that has made His Spirit to understand the Book.

But I am going to talk to you this morning about the faith that is here spoken of. We have been talking about faith ever since the Lord came. It is not exhausted yet; and God forbid that I should know yet what faith is; although I know a little what it is. I think the meaning of the phrase is this: Faith is the foundation, the root, the underlying substance of hope. If you have any hope, it comes from some faith in you. Hope, you may say, is a bud upon the plant of faith, a bud from the root of faith; the flower is joy and peace.

163

Now the evidence of things not seen—I cannot, as I say, find any meaning in that at all; but the true meaning is the most profound fact in human history; it is the trial or the proving of things not seen.

Now upon that turns the life of every man, especially, perhaps, in the present day. This thing of faith means the whole recognized fellowship of man to God and His fellows; it is the right position of the human soul which is made to understand the truth— the right position of that soul towards the truth; that is faith, partly. But you must remember that whenever you begin to speak of anything true, divine, heavenly, beyond the human, you cannot speak of it at all without speaking in some measure wrongly about it. We have no words, we have no phrases, we have no possible combination of sentences—nay, we have no forms of intellect that do more than represent fragmentarily the greatness of the things that belongs to the very vital being of our nature. Much, much foolish talk has been uttered about faith. Oh, this talking, friends. I would not trouble myself to set your opinions all right from this moment, henceforth, and for ever. I would not get up into the pulpit and do so. I do not think it is worth any man's labour; but if I could stir up a single soul, instead of talking about the meaning even of the greatest things, to go and do the smallest duty, I should say that is the kind of duty for which Christ spent Himself. If you read His life wisely you will see that His constant effort is to turn a man's thought back to himself, and make him do a thing, and not talk about it. About faith they often used to say that it was antithetically opposed to works.

There never was greater nonsense. They would say that Paul taught faith and St. James taught works—and indeed one would feel something like this sometimes—that St. Paul had gone too far and that St. James had to write that epistle to set him right. It is not any of us, friends, that will find St. Paul or St. James wrong, nor was there the smallest difference between them. On the contrary, I assert that faith is simply the greatest work that man can do. Taking it in its

164

simplest, original development, it is the highest effort of the whole human intellect, imagination, will, in the highest direction. Never does the human nature put forth itself in such power, with such effort, with such energy as to have faith in God. I say it is the highest, and sometimes the most difficult, work that a man can do.

Then, that is attended by thousands and thousands of other works of faith. In the present state of England's history—and we may add that of several other countries to it—it seems as if it were more difficult to believe than ever it was before. It seems also—I may say seems—it seems also to many people, and some people in certain moods, as if there was less faith in the world than ever there was before. And when they look in their own hearts—even those who would feign rank themselves among believers they recognise there an amount of doubt, difficulty, and fear that appals themselves. What?! Is the whole thing going to vanish like "the baseless fabric of a vision"?—all this story of Christ, His life and death, and the conquests that were made in His name—is it all going out of sight; and are we to be left where the world was before He came?

I should like to help some of you, if I can, friends, about all this. It troubles some of your hearts; and some of you, perhaps, ought to be a little more troubled about it than you are, because it lies at your door in some measure; but I should like if, ,on the minds of young men particularly—although there is sad enough ground for including young women, too—if I could impress upon them that, let the thing look to them as it may, it is a notion and a false idea of Christianity that has come into their minds, partly because their own doors were opened narrow, partly because their own aspirations were so low, partly because they have been so little in earnest for the truth; it is about to vanish away and must perish; but the true thing—God's notion of it; what Christ thought and felt while He was here; what He thinks and feels now when He is here still—is that which shall never pass away but is the true fountain of truth and life to

165

all the generations.

But first of all let me say a word to the man or woman who is troubled with the difficulty of believing. Now-a-days, there is such a talk about science, and such a contempt poured forth on the man who thinks to walk without that kind of science for the guide of his life, who has a different goal, a different ambition, whose thoughts stretch further than the things of this life—the things he sees and hears and handles—if there be such a man among us, friends, who does the work of the world, and does it well, but his head is in heaven—that is the kind of thing we ought all to be an to seek. And there are perhaps a few even now of this kind, and there are more growing. But let me say to you about your own fears and doubts and difficulties—it is a great thing to believe. Are you fit to believe? I have just said that I believe it to be the loftiest exercise of the human being and of human nature. How can you expect to believe?

Are you like Nathanial—an Israelite indeed, a man without guile? What are your ways? What have you been about? What are your desires in life? How have you been ordering yourself? If it may be that although the power of God upon you makes you feel that you ought to believe, that you are such that you cannot believe, and it is your own fault. Fully do I recognise the difficulty. I question if there is a doubt or a sense of difficulty that prevails now that has not passed through my own mind as a thing to be encountered and understood and settled. It is natural that we should doubt, with such cries especially on all sides of us, and the intellect so much more awake than ever it was before, and indeed the conscience not more asleep than before; and with one on this side and one on that side crying out, "I have reached, I have seen, and I have found no God." Settle this with yourselves to begin with. Not all the intellect or metaphysics of the world could prove that there is no God, and not all the intellect in the world could prove that there is a God. If you could prove that there is a God, that would imply that you could go all around Him, and buttress up his being with your human argument that He should exist. As soon might a child on his mother's bosom, looking up into his mother's face, write a treatise on what a woman was and what a mother was.

But do not think that God is angry with you because you find it hard to believe. It is not so; that is not like God; God is all that you can honestly wish Him to be, and infinitely more; He is not angry with you for that. And He knows perfectly well what the scientific man calls truth—although you will observe that he is always constantly, and everywhere changing his theories—that what the scientific man calls truth is simply an impossibility with regard to God; And God knows it. Your brain, the symbol of your intellect, cannot, concerning Him, if He exists, receive that kind of proof which you have when you read a proposition of Euclid. It commends itself to your mind and your understanding. You say, "So it is, and it cannot be otherwise." But you cannot receive that kind of; there is no such proof with regard to the Mighty God.

And therefore I say if you doubt the existence of the living God, He is not angry with you for that. But I am speaking of those who would fain believe if they could, I ask you, have you been trying the things not seen? Have you been proving them? This is what God puts in your hands. He says, " I tell you I Am. You act upon that; for I know that your conscience moves you to it; you act upon that and you will find whether I Am or not, and what I Am." Do you see? Faith in its true sense does not belong to the intellect alone, nor to the intellect first, but to the conscience, to the will, and that man is a faithful man who says "I cannot prove that there is a God, but, O God, if Thou hearest me anywhere, help me to do Thy will." There is faith, "Do this," and he does it. It is o, friends, that is faith; it is doing that thing which you, let me say, even only suppose to be the will of God; for if you are wrong, and do it because you think it is His will, He will set you right. It is the turning of the eye to the light; it is the sending of the feet into the path that is

167

required, putting the hands to do the things which the conscience says ought to be done.

You will notice that all this chapter from which I have taken the text is a list of people that did things. Some of them were made kings, and some of them were sawn asunder for it; but it was all for faith, and nothing but faith. There was a truth; there was a live truth; a truth that had welled through and called the knowledge of truth up in us, nay, called up in us the very possibility of feeling truth; and according to this law these men walked through all the world, and all the worlds together set themselves against them, and in the name of the original vital law of the universe— namely, the living God—they walked right on and met their fate. Yes; victory and the participation of the Divine nature, that was their faith.

Therefore, friends, the practical thing is just this, and it is the one lesson that we have to learn, that whatever our doubts or difficulties, we must do the thing we know in order to learn the thing we do not know; but whether we learn it or not, "If ye know these things," saith the Master, "happy are ye if you do them." It is the doing that is everything, and the doing is faith and there is no division between them.

Then I would say a word to those who are further on. They have been trying to serve God for many years now, they do not seem to themselves to have made much of it. They find that they are still troubled in their soul—not whether they be of God; but does he manage everything now? "Where is He? I have never seen Him; if He would but speak to myself! I have been crying for Him for all these years, and I have never had a sign out of the great blank. Oh, if He would but show Himself; if He would but do something—give me the meanest sign that He actually is, and that He cares about me." You say, "I feel as if I could go and on for ever then." Friends, I believe there is no sign God could give you, but what you would begin to doubt again. I do not believe there is any miracle He could work before your eyes even, that by-and-by you would not begin to doubt, and be just as lost as before. God will not give us little things to spoil our appetite for great things. God will never be content until we are one with Him as He is one with Christ; God will not give us signs and wonders and these inferior things, for be sure God's common and usual way is far better than His miraculous way, as we call it; If it were all miracle, we would make it all common. You may be sure then, that God's usual way of doing things is the best way. I say He will not give us signs of anything outside to give us confidence in Him.

Nothing will serve God turn but this—that our faith in Him shall be complete, go instantly with our perception of what He is. It is by the vision in our souls, the feeling and perception in our souls of what God is, that we are able to believe in Him. Let a man once see God as Christ saw Him, and he believes. He does not see Him perfectly, and his faith will never be absolutely complete until he comes to that point when he recognises the character and being and relation of God to himself; and then he believes; and any glimmer of the truth in regard to our Lord's nature helps us to believe—enables us to go on, and on, and on; So that you see that the same thing that the intellect does with Euclid, the whole mind, heart, intellect, imagination, conscience, and will does with regard to God when a man sees God and knows Him. The man says, "I know enough to make life a grand and blessed and strong thing to me, and I am going on." We will see. "I cannot convey to you," he may say, "my conviction; that will only come with the conviction itself; you must see, else you do not know; but life to me is enough." So would he say; but then, "What is the way to this?" you say. Ah! my friends, if you have been at it for twenty or thirty or forty years, surely you have learnt by this time what you have just to go on doing—that is hearkening to Christ and doing His will. Let me try you a bit.

What is your first thought in the morning? Is it "God is life"? or is it "How am I to order my day's work?" Is it "God is very rich and I am His child and He will see to me"? or is it "How on earth shall I get through this that lies before me?" Are you afraid? Are the cares of this world troublesome to you? Well, you have not got on much. But if you are not trying to suppress them, if you are not trying to get rid of them, I am afraid you have not got on at all; and if you had been thirty or forty years trying to serve Christ, it has been a kind of service that He does not care much about, and it is no wonder that you do not get on. You have been very careful reading your Bible and going to church, and this thing and that thing that you think belongs to religion; but have you been doing the thing Christ told you?

If you do that, I do not care whatever else you do; you cannot be wrong then. The same holds with you as with the beginner who is troubled as to whether there is a God or not. But you that believe in a God do not trust Him; whereas, the other is not sure that there is a God; and you think it very horrible of him to doubt the existence of a God. And yet you, believing that there is a God, are afraid of the trouble, the poverty, the opinion of the world, and are ambitious to get on this way or that! Oh, had almost sooner say you do not believe in a God than say that you believe in God, and yet He is nothing to you. And when you feel inclined to say heavy and hard things about your atheistic neighbour, think that there may be a beam in your own eye even worse—if we can bear to call it so—than the mote in his. Indeed, friends, it is because our life does not shine that men have stood up and said "There is no light." You see a man greedy and grasping—as much taken up with the things of this world as if he were to live—I will not say to the age of Methusaleh—but to the age of seventy-five or eighty. He works in the world as if he were to live for ever in it; and sometimes, I think, the punishment that would fit him best would be to be condemned to live for ever in the world.

What a thing that would be! Ah!, the man who is most sure that there is no God and that he can get on pretty well—he won't say first rate—but pretty well without Him; I think the better way would be just to let him live on and on and on, until he got heartily sick of himself and hated himself, and would gladly yield anything to get out of himself. Ah, friends, there is a worse thing than dying never to wake again. There is a worse thing than dying for ever, and going soul and brain to the dust, and that is to wake up and find that there is no God. That is the horror of horrors to me. But to tell me that I am to live for ever, and that there is no God! For anything any man knows who does not believe in a God it may be so. He cannot tell with certainty that he is going to die forever because he sees no more of those that have gone before. Why should not they go on to some other sphere as they came into this one? Without any warning or any choice, they do not know until they find themselves here. Why should it not be so in another state of existence? But to find yourselves there without a God! There is no use praying to be killed, because there is no |God to hear your prayer. You can no more annihilate yourselves than make yourselves; the whole thing would be utter misery, especially when the man has such ideas that he is satisfied with himself. But what is to be done with you and me, who cannot finish ourselves? Poor creatures! we feel that if God is like us, He had better cease and we had better all cease; but if we see He is like us—only He is perfect, absolute in grandeur and loveliness, ah then, "I shall get rid of this bad in me—this poor, mean stuff in me, and I shall become glorious, true, and excellent like Him."

That is worth living for; nothing else is; it is for that that Christ tells us to put confidence in Him and obey His word, and we shall see the Father. "He that heareth and openeth the door, I will come in, sit down with him, and sup with him and he with Me." When God is seated at the very fireside of our hearts, then there is no more doubt. I say, friends, it is a good thing that you should have doubt until you see that nothing less than that will do, and until you come to desire that, and to turn your judgments, your thought, and feeling in that direction. Oh! friends; I know nothing else in the world worth knowing. I could go on talking to you all the day long about this, but I should weary you. Faith is the trying of the things unseen—the putting them to the test, and whatever your doubts or your fears are try Him by obedience, and then you will get help to carry you on. Less than that won't do. The darkness of life's closing time will come round about you, and find you very doubtful, very sad, looking, looking into the darkness and wondering "Shall I wake or shall I sleep?" But if you believe that that man died and rose again, the whole thing is full of the dawn of an eternal morning. Coming up beyond the hills of this life, and full of such hope as the highest imagination of the poet has not a glimmer as of yet.

Do you hope for anything, friends? Thank God, that comes from you faith. No man that has not faith can hope. But do not think the world is going all to the devil. There is a better and stronger faith coming. It was a great thing that this foolish, actionless kind of religion should vanish, and that a simple, obedient, hoping, trusting life should takes its place. The world is not worse than it was. Many even of those that do not believe in God have faith towards their neighbour. Even those who do not believe, on the whole are better in this century than those that did not believe in the last. Only, we are a set of foolish men and women who simply talk and nothing else—neither believe nor disbelieve—who have neither the soul nor the heart to be in earnest about anything. God has a hold upon them too, and He has but to place His hand upon them to make them feel it.

But, friends, what we have to do is let our light shine. Do you get any light? Let it shine. I do not mean be an example to other people. You have no business to set yourselves up for an example; you have to be and to do, and that is letting the light shine. It ought not to be possible to mistake a Christian for a man of the world. His very dealings with every man that comes near him have something to show, something that Christ would have done that a man of the world would not do. Tell me how you would like Christ to come in upon you at any moment in the midst of your business talk. Would you be ready to turn to Him and say,

"Master, this is how I am saying the thing to my friend; this is how I see it in the light of Thy love!"? Would you be ready for that, or do you think that a great part of your being and your life can be conducted upon other laws than Christian? If a man does that, he is altogether wrong—altogether wrong. Christ is God, the all-in-all, or nothing at all. If we were as the bush—if every Christian were as the bush that burned with fire—that would be the shining our light before men. Atheism would soon vanish; unbelief would draw in its horns; reproved, judged, condemned by the very presence of faith.

I would have you, then, friends, remember that faith is the trying of the thing that you do not see, and that you cannot be sure about, a thing that you do not see and which, not seeing, you have doubt about, you can yet try—that is faith; and if you are honest, that will be a great opportunity and a great help to you; it will start a fresh faith which you have not thought of before, and give your life a new start. Faith is intended to put to the test the unseen world of truth, love, law, hope, redemption. God grant us all faith enough to carry on from point to point till the faith shall vanish into light, and we have never to think about faith more, nor to think about Church more, nor the Bible more, nor prayer more, but our whole being shall be a delighted consciousness of the presence of God and His Christ.

NOTES:[32]

---

[32] v 1.1 --- 3/16/16

www.ingramcontent.com/pod-product-compliance
Lightning Source LLC
LaVergne TN
LVHW021447080426
835509LV00018B/2195